Puppy Training Book

Training the Best Dog Ever
The Beginner's Guide to Training a
Puppy with Dog Training Basics
The Puppy Training Handbook

Table of Contents

Introduction 1

Chapter 1: Before Bringing Your Puppy Home 3

Chapter 2: A Happy Home 22

Chapter 3: Training Your Puppy 31

Chapter 4: Dealing with Behavioral Problems 61

Chapter 5: Grooming Your Puppy 94

    Location 95

    Getting your dog used to toothbrushing 100

    What tools to get 101

   Important points 105

Chapter 6: Doctor at Home 108

Conclusion 133

© Copyright 2019 by ___ - All rights reserved.

This document is geared towards providing exact and reliable information in regards to the topic and issue covered. The publication is sold with the idea that the publisher is not required to render accounting, officially permitted, or otherwise, qualified services. If advice is necessary, legal or professional, a practiced individual in the profession should be ordered.

- From a Declaration of Principles which was accepted and approved equally by a Committee of the American Bar Association and a Committee of Publishers and Associations.

In no way is it legal to reproduce, duplicate, or transmit any part of this document in either electronic means or in printed format. Recording of this publication is strictly prohibited and any storage of this document is not allowed unless with written permission from the publisher. All rights reserved.

The information provided herein is stated to be truthful and consistent, in that any liability, in terms of inattention or otherwise, by any usage or abuse of any policies, processes, or directions contained within is the solitary and utter responsibility of the recipient reader. Under no circumstances will any legal responsibility or blame be held against the publisher for any reparation, damages, or monetary

loss due to the information herein, either directly or indirectly.
Respective authors own all copyrights not held by the publisher.

The information herein is offered for informational purposes solely, and is universal as so. The presentation of the information is without contract or any type of guarantee assurance.

The trademarks that are used are without any consent, and the publication of the trademark is without permission or backing by the trademark owner. All trademarks and brands within this book are for clarifying purposes only and are the owned by the owners themselves, not affiliated with this document.

Introduction

Introduction

Congratulations, you've adopted a puppy! You're probably very excited about your new family member and all the perks that come with being a puppy parent! However, you need to be prepared for the upcoming responsibilities as it's no walk in the park. In order for your pup to grow into a happy, healthy and confident dog, you'll need to understand what goes into raising one.

Dogs primarily make the perfect pets for families, so if you're single, you might want to reconsider your options for a pet companion before you adopt a puppy. Dogs will demand a lot of your attention, or else they may grow to be misbehaved and irritable.

Just like their human companions, dogs have very complex psyches. If they're not exposed to enough affection in early stages, this can be detrimental to their mental health. A balanced feeding and a spacious backyard is not enough for a dog to be happy. That said, if you live in an apartment with no access to a spacious garden, then owning a dog will be more challenging for you and less convenient for your pet.

So, before you get a dog, make sure you understand that it is not going to be a walk in the park—pun intended—and that you are ready to put in the work it requires.

Chapter 1: Before Bringing Your Puppy Home

Bringing a new puppy home is a delightful treat for the whole family, one that can significantly brighten everyone's day. Since granting a safe and loving home for a puppy is no small feat, there are a few things to consider ahead of time. Puppies are tiny, defenseless, and far away from their mother, so they need extra care and a watchful eye to ensure that they grow healthfully. You might be a bit overwhelmed and confused as to how exactly you should go about doing so, and it's only natural that you feel this way. With some research and careful planning, though, you'll surely become a skillful fur-parent in no time.

Can You Afford a Puppy?
Looking at the picture of owning a dog from an outsider's perspective might not reflect the truth, especially regarding the expenses. So, before you make the decision, consider all the following costs of having a puppy and decide whether you can actually afford one.

Upfront costs
When it comes to dogs, the range of prices can vary immensely depending on two main factors: the breed and whether you're buying or adopting. Because some breeds are rare or are purchased for specific purposes, the initial cost can be quite high; however, there is always the option of adopting a dog from the nearest shelter. The advantage is that, in most cases, you won't actually pay anything—or you'll pay a minimal amount and you'll be giving a homeless dog a forever home.

Vaccines and microchipping
Another upfront cost to take into consideration after getting a dog is paying for the necessary vaccines. Depending on what it's already taken, how old it is and which season you're in, there will be different vaccines available, but in any case, it is a cost that you should take into account. Getting your puppy microchipped is another essential upfront, one-time cost to prove ownership if your dog is lost, and it's a must if you're ever planning to travel abroad. While these costs might initially add up since they usually emerge at the same time, they are only paid once. It is also worth mentioning that

adopting a dog from a shelter can sometimes minimize the initial expenses as they tend to already be vaccinated and microchipped.

Bedding, collar and toys
When considering initial costs, don't forget that you'll also need to purchase a comfortable place for the newest member of your family to sleep in. You'll need a collar and leash for when you take your dog out for a walk and a few toys to keep it entertained, especially while it's home alone—this can actually stop it from ruining your furniture out of boredom, too. While you're at it, you should also get a name tag with your name and number on it, just in case your furball ends up getting lost.

Dog food
Depending on the size and activity level of your dog, the amount of food it'll consume will also vary. On average, a young, medium-sized dog will go through 30 pounds of dry dog food in six to eight weeks. If you choose to feed your pup raw or home-cooked meals, you need to calculate those costs as well.

Vet care

Don't forget to take into consideration frequent visits to the vet and also assume that just like little babies, puppies also tend to get sick and will need to be taken to a vet, which could really add up to the overall costs of taking care of a puppy.

It is important to remember that puppies require proper care and come with their own set of expenses that you need to be prepared for. Taking all these costs into account will allow you to properly budget for your newest family member. And if you're still in the decision phase, carefully studying all these points can give you an idea of whether you can really afford a puppy or not, before you take on the responsibility and end up getting alarmed by the amount of expenses you need to cover.

What You Need to Get
Owning a dog is not cheap, so that's one thing you need to consider before adopting a pet. And while many households can afford to get a dog, only a few have extra time on their hands to invest in a new family member. Unlike their feline counterparts, canines need plenty of attention, especially if they're still in their nurturing phase.

However, if you think you have extra time and money on your hands to finally adopt a puppy, here's what you need to get before your trip to the shelter.

Dog-proof fence
Canines are naturally curious creatures. The good news is, if they ever find their way out, they'll likely be able to follow the scent back home. However, there's plenty to worry about beyond the fence of your home that could seriously injure your dog, and in some extreme cases, result in its death.

If you don't have a fence right now, don't bring your dog home in the hope of keeping it as a strictly indoor pet. Even if you walk your dog every morning, you're still going to want it to wander about in your yard for some moderate sun exposure, and to give it extra space to explore and get enough exercise without having to be on a leash.

Dogs also tend to get bored easily, so access to the backyard will allow them to watch your neighbors and maybe even chase some squirrels. Don't worry, it's unlikely that they'll catch any of them.

Just make sure you limit your dog's access to open spaces to daytime, as it will likely bark at passing pedestrians, which can be disturbing to your neighbors at nighttime.

Another reason you want to get a fence is that it allows your best friend to freely get frequent bathroom breaks. This is especially important when it's still a puppy; you'll have to teach it where it's okay to go potty, or else you'll have a lot to clean up on a daily basis.

Just remember that getting a fence does not replace taking your dog on a walk. Dogs need to be walked every day for a change of scenery, an adequate amount of exercise, and some mental stimulation. This also helps you bond with your new puppy and gives it something to look forward to every day.

Pet gates

Whether you're adopting a young pup or opting for a senior dog, you're going to have to keep the nosy little furball away from parts of your home that could be dangerous for it to explore, or any other place that you'd like to keep clean and tidy. Canines are curious and messy, and any room they access may end up being subject to a few chewed up objects or broken vases.

There are gates specifically designed for pets, but some are so low that your puppy can learn to leap over them. Make sure the gates you go for are both high and sturdy enough.

We recommend you get these installed at multiple entrances; although, you shouldn't keep them closed at all times. They can be a great way to discipline your dog not to interrupt you while you're cooking or eating. For the first few months, expect your dog to bark and wail at the closed gate. It *will* be heartbreaking, but eventually, your dog will learn when and where it can access areas in your home.

The possibilities are endless when it comes to where you can install pet gates, but we would advise against overusing them. Dogs expect to be treated as part of the family. If you restrict their access to multiple areas for prolonged periods of time, this also limits the time you spend with your dog, which can take a toll on their mental health. Use the gates in moderation, when you absolutely have to.

Chew toys

Think of chew toys as pacifiers for babies. In their teething phase, puppies will either chew on the numerous toys that you provide them, or they'll chew holes through your furniture. There's no third option.

Chewing for growing puppies is akin to an itch that needs to be scratched, and it helps them grow healthy teeth quickly. However, that's not to say that fully-grown dogs will stop using their chew toys. Wild canines naturally exert a lot of effort while chewing through the flesh and bones of their prey—a natural instinct that canned or dry food does not satiate. Because your dog doesn't go out to hunt, it needs to find something else to chew on other than prey.

Your options are endless, and preferences fully depend on your dog. Most canines, especially puppies, enjoy squeaky toys because they mimic squealing prey. It may sound gruesome, but it's only instinct. You'll most likely want to provide your puppy with a variety of toys to choose from. Bigger plush toys will be their favorite to occasionally chew on, and also use as snuggle pillows when they nap. Bone-shaped squeaky toys are usually great distractions to pass the time, or to enjoy some quality playtime with you. If you'll leave your dog unaccompanied for a few hours, the best toy to keep it entertained with is a rubber chew treat toy, which can be filled with treats that ooze out of the toy when bit or squeezed. This also mimics a hunting experience, which will keep your dog's instincts satiated, and will, in turn, help keep your pet well-behaved.

There are also flavored toys, which double as toothbrushes for your pup. These toys are specially designed with soft bristles that clean your dog's teeth as it chews on the toy. They're great for some extra dental care, but don't forget that they can't replace a thorough toothbrushing routine. Some canines are also finicky when it comes to cheap rubber that smells artificial. Opt for a flavored toy to make it more appealing to your dog.

Food and water accessories
You should invest in some sturdy and easy-to-clean food and water bowls as soon as you can. Growing puppies have enormous appetites and you need to make sure that you have the right tools on hand to feed them regularly. It's advisable to get a fairly large water bowl, too, as all dogs need easy access to clean, fresh water at all times.

Furthermore, you should put your puppy on a diet recommended by the vet as he or she might want to modify their meal plans according to any specific concerns or ailments currently aggravating your puppy.

An automatic food dispenser will be your best friend (aside from your furry companion) if you spend long hours at work every day. Even if you feed your dog as soon as you get back home, it's best to schedule timed feedings for your pet, especially since dogs truly thrive on routine.

Many dog feeders can be timed to regulate your pet's eating schedule, and you get to choose how much you want to feed on a daily basis, as well. This will also help if your dog tends to wake you up early in the morning, demanding to be fed.

Feeders can work with wet or dry food depending on the model, and different brands cater to different sizes.

Timed 12-meal automatic feeders are considered the best and healthiest option for small or medium-sized dogs. This way, instead of eating two big meals, they're fed 12 smaller meals throughout the day. The slow feed mode slowly dispenses food over the course of 15 minutes to prevent your dog from vomiting, which usually happens when dogs eat too quickly.

But that doesn't mean that the machine gets to pick when and how your dog eats. If you want to set an eating schedule for your dog on your own terms for medical reasons, there's an immediate feed mode that allows you to select the portion of food served as well.

For bigger dogs, 5-meal feeders can be set to serve more generous portions, and whatever schedule you choose automatically rotates to the following day. Unlike its 12-meal counterpart, this dispenser works great with dry as well as wet food.

Whatever dispenser you choose for your dog, make sure you take out the tray or bowl to clean it every day.

Dog house

Dogs should always be allowed to come inside whenever they want to, but if they regularly spend time in your backyard (and they probably will), it's best to install a comfortable dog house for them.

For starters, this creates a space for them that they feel is their own. Just like your household members have a room of their own, a dog house will be your pet's personal space. Dog houses can also protect your pets from heat strokes; however, if it's even moderately hot for you outside, it's likely too hot for your dog. Make sure that whatever dog door you have installed can be locked when necessary, so you can keep your buddy indoors when the weather conditions are not ideal.

You don't have to spend hundreds of dollars on custom-made dog houses that match the exterior design of your home. Any generic den made of white cedar will be quite durable, and also safe for your dog. White cedar is also known as stained white wood, and the reason why it makes the perfect material for dog houses is that it's naturally non-toxic for pets and gives off a pleasing scent even when wet.

Aside from being an aesthetically pleasing addition to your yard, it's also resistant to severe weather changes as well as pests that may infest your garden, so you can rest assured that your dog will be safe under its little sloped roof.

If you're going to make your purchase online, make sure you select the correct size. If you plan on adopting a pup, bigger sizes are unnecessary. Dogs, in general, enjoy cozy spaces, so anything too commodious for your fur baby is not recommended. Whatever you pick, we recommend you get one with floor panels, so your dog doesn't have to take a nap on a wet lawn.

Grooming kit

You should at least have a basic grooming kit at home, even if you plan to regularly take your dog to a professional groomer.

Grooming isn't just about keeping your dog looking adorable. Trimming a dog's fur and nails regularly is sanitary and helps you spot any signs of potential infections or illnesses. Grooming your pet regularly will also minimize coat and skin issues like consistent scratching, rashes, bumps, and matting. Combing your dog's hair evenly distributes hair oils, which means your dog will have a healthier and shinier coat.

Grooming is also healthier for the dog's human companion as it cuts down on allergens like shed hair.

Your kit should usually have a comb, scissors, trimmers, and clippers. Depending on the breed, many dogs will be particularly scared of loud clippers. There are many silent ones on the market specifically created for timid puppies. If you're unsure if your dog will take grooming well, go for the silent kit, and remember that its perception of this experience can always be improved with lots of love, praise, and treats.

Before grooming, make sure your dog is bathed. If your dog regularly plays outside, a weekly bath should suffice. Do not bathe your dog more than once weekly.

If your puppy has a thick coat, untangle any knots before you bathe it. Use lukewarm water and diluted dog shampoo. Never use soap or human shampoo on dogs, although some people may choose to use horse shampoo for thicker and shinier coats.

With certain breeds, you'll want to invest in a stripping knife. Dogs that do not naturally shed hair will need you to manually strip overgrown and dead hair. Make sure your dog is comfortable with being stripped, or else this process will be extremely inconvenient for both you and your pet.

Use nail clippers to keep your dog's nails trimmed. If you don't cut them regularly, they'll be more difficult to cut the next time you try to do it. Standard scissors work fine, but we recommend the guillotine clipper. If you skip this step, it will become increasingly difficult for your dog to walk, as their nails will grow into a curve that pricks at their paws as they move around.

Aside from trimming nails and hair, make sure you regularly comb your dog to remove any shed hair and keep its coat clean and tangle-free.

Collars and leashes

Although they may be the most obvious ones on the list, they're definitely essential items regardless of where you're keeping your puppy until it grows up. Walking your puppy can help the two of you bond, and will make it grow to be more comfortable around humans.

When it comes to collars, ID tags are essential to make sure that your pet will always be identified in case it loses its way. Puppies are generally hyperactive and fun-loving, so make sure that your leash is a good fit; otherwise, you may suddenly lose your grip if your puppy sees a familiar neighbor in the distance, or a stray animal it wants to chase.

No matter what kind of leash or collar you get your dog, though, nothing will be as safe as getting it microchipped, which will allow you to find out exactly where it is. If a microchipped dog ever gets lost and someone takes it to a vet, they will use your information to contact you and bring your dog back.

When picking collars, make sure it's the right fit. Collars that are too tight can be extremely uncomfortable for your dog, while others may slip off easily. Whatever you choose, make sure that you have extras lying around so you can easily replace them if they get lost.

Carrier

Carriers for bigger dogs are tricky business, but it's nothing that your local pet shop cannot guide you through. Your puppy will likely fit in any plastic carrier, but as your dog grows up, you'll find yourself switching between bigger sizes.

You should always know the weight and measurements of your dog before you head to a pet shop. Measure your dog from the base of its neck to the root of its tail, then add a few inches for the head and tail. The height should also be calculated, and the weight of your dog contributes to the material you'll opt for to make sure it's sturdy enough for your dog's size.

There are plastic and wooden carriers, as well as soft-sided ones. It all depends on how you plan to use them. If you're on your way to a flight, soft-sided carriers can easily be placed under seats. But if your dog is traveling in cargo, make sure the carrier is hard, sturdy, and most importantly, well-ventilated.

If you're using your carrier for vet trips, backpack carriers work great for smaller puppies. Bigger dogs can easily be carried to a car or taken on public transportation.

Whatever carrier you buy, make sure it is durable. If you cheap out on your pet shopping spree, you might end up repurchasing everything. Bear in mind that dogs can easily escape cheap fabric carriers.

Dog bed

It doesn't matter if you plan to have your dog sleep next to you; your pet should always have a bed of its own. Just like dog houses, dog beds are part of your best friend's personal bubble. And the fact is, dogs will likely choose their own beds over yours.

There are plenty of dog beds out there, and each depends on the sleeping style of your dog. You can get a sprawler, a burrower, a curler, or a leaner. Shape and design aside, you need to make sure that you purchase the correct size, which isn't too spacious or too small for your dog.

You'll find different fabrics on the market. Most of them don't make a difference, as long as you check the label or description of the product and make sure that it's machine-washable, bearing in mind that dog beds will need to be washed regularly.

Piddle pads and newspapers
Unfortunately, some dogs can be hard to train, and the first few weeks at your home will probably be a bit of a nightmare. Adding to that is the fact that puppies tend to leak, so you'll need to keep your home stocked with all sorts of training pads and line the floors with newspapers until your pet gets the lay of the

land. While you're at it, you might like to cover your couches and beds in vinyl because chances are, your new bundle of cuteness will involuntarily wet them, so it's best to err on the side of caution.

A veterinarian

While that's not something you can get at the store, it's something you need to be prepared for before you adopt a new puppy.

Some people tend to think of vet centers as places your pet only needs to visit when it's ill. But the fact is, you're going to have to invest in monthly visits for regular check-ups. Even if your dog is acting the same, there's a ton of medical complications that can be detected by your vet, preferably at early stages.

There are also times when your dog may *seem* okay, but is actually enduring an ache, allergies, or a developing infection.

That said, your dog will have to be regularly dewormed and will eventually have to be neutered or spayed, if this hasn't already been done by the shelter. Ask the rescuer of your puppy if it has already been vaccinated so your vet knows what he/she is dealing with.

Don't just pick the closest vet to your home. Make sure you check reviews before you decide to trust a vet with your puppy. If taking your dog to the vet is too much of a hassle, home visits are also an option, but can be fairly more expensive.

Even though getting a dog might sound like a heartwarming idea, it's also a huge responsibility. So, before you make the big decision, make sure that your work schedule allows you to invest in bringing up a puppy. And if this is the first pet you own, be sure to contact your local vet before you bring your dog home, to be made aware of the check-ups you'll have to make to keep your dog happy and healthy.

Chapter 2: A Happy Home

Now that you've made the big decision and prepared your house or apartment for your new fur baby, the next step is to make sure it gets accustomed to its surroundings as soon as possible, and makes itself at home! In order to achieve this, you'll have to decide on a few key points regarding its diet and routine, and form a certain bond with your pup. In time, both of you will get a better understanding of how things will be working around your place, but for now, you can start by focusing on your dog's nutrition and its way of communicating with you, so as not to miss any important signs it might be giving you regarding its happiness and well-being.

How and When to Feed Your Puppy
Once you have a joyful little pooch constantly giving you the puppy eyes for the next mealtime, you'll realize how important it is that you know what it should be eating, and how often you should feed it. So, here's a feeding guide to help you wrap your head around it.

What should you feed your puppy?
When it comes to commercial food, you'll find canned or semi-moist food, or kibble. When

deciding which one your puppy should be eating, it is best to not only know what it was previously feeding on, but also what the vet recommends for its nutritional requirements. It is worth noting that kibble is usually the most economical and practical option, but some dogs are prone to be allergic to some of the components. If you're changing from one type to another, it is best to make the change gradually, so it's easy on the puppy's stomach and doesn't lead to digestion problems.

Wet food vs dry food
The dilemma of whether to opt for wet or dry food is real. But, in order to make a calculated decision, you should first understand why each one is important for your puppy. It is worth mentioning that depending on the specific brand of dog food you'll be purchasing, the ingredients and nutrients it contains, as well as its consistency may differ dramatically. That said, each type does come with some advantages.

Wet food
While wet food is usually more expensive, it can be more beneficial for your dog. You'll notice that wet food is more intense in smell because it has a stronger taste, making it preferred by dogs

to dry food if they were given a choice. Another important difference is that since wet food has a lot more liquid in it, it can make up for some of your dog's required water intake. So, if your dog has trouble drinking water, then it is recommended to feed it wet food—though dehydration is a major issue in dogs, so don't depend merely on the moisture content of canned food. For dogs that have a tendency to overeat and become overweight, wet food will also be a better option as it has a lower amount of energy content, which allows them to eat more without exceeding their calorie intake.

If kibble is not really your thing but the cost of buying wet food for the rest of your dog's life also seems a bit overwhelming, you can also prepare fresh, homemade meals for your furry friend. In that case, you can feed it a raw diet, which has many proven health benefits, or do some research to find some balanced, home-cooked dog food recipes online.

Dry food

You'll find that the average type of kibble tends to be cheaper than wet food. You'll also find a wide variety of options that will help you choose the best for your dog. Another aspect to consider is that since dry food is actually dry, it doesn't go bad as fast as wet food and can be left out while you're at work or traveling without you having to worry. Dry food also usually contains a higher amount of energy sources, which means a smaller quantity is needed in order to meet the dog's daily food intake requirements. You'll notice that dry food usually has a less distinct smell, making it more convenient to leave out without the entire house smelling like dog food. However, if you have a picky eater, you might have to enhance the smell and flavor by adding some chicken broth or some "toppers" to its food.

When it comes to dry food, you'll find a variety of options with a wide range of prices. While you might be tempted to go for the cheapest option, consider the fact that the price varies according to the quality of the ingredients. So, in order to ensure that your puppy is getting the nutrients it needs, it is best to pick at least a mid-range brand to guarantee that it gets the required nutrition without spending too much money. No matter which type of food or brand you decide on, don't forget to carefully read the labels, and better yet, consult with your vet.

What nutrients are important for your puppy?
Always double-check the ingredients to make sure that they are rich in protein in order to help support your puppy's muscles and growth. It is also important to have carbohydrates included in the diet, as it supplies the puppy with the energy needed to play and be active. Calcium is another crucial ingredient as it supports the development of teeth and bones, especially when a whelp is still growing, and omega-3 fatty acids are essential in order to maintain a healthy brain, heart, kidney, and coat, in addition to strengthening the immune system.

How often should you feed your puppy?
Depending on the size and age of your furball, the feeding schedule will differ.

6-12 weeks
During this time, a puppy needs to be feeding more frequently in order to ensure growth and that's why it is best to feed it around four times per day. However, it is vital to choose food that the puppy's stomach can digest, so you need to choose a type of dog food that's specially designed for puppies.

3-6 months
Once your puppy has grown and has started developing, it is time to decrease the number of times it eats and bring it down to three times a day instead.

6-12 months
If you've noticed your puppy is growing healthily into a little doggie, then it is recommended to only feed it twice a day. You can offer one portion of dog food before you leave the house in the morning and refill for a second serving once you get back. This should be enough food for your dog, but you'll be able to tell by the constant whimpering if it gets hungry more frequently and is in need of a higher dosage. During this period, it is also recommended to switch from puppy to adult food, at around eight months if you have a small breed. However, if you have a larger breed, then it is best to wait until it turns 13 months to switch to adult food.

When it comes to nutrition, it is always important to get a consultation from your vet to help you determine what type of food your dog not only needs, but will benefit from the most. It may take some trial and error at first, but don't worry—as long as you know how to look for all the signs, your pup will tell you whether its current diet seems to be working for it or not.

Stress Signals You Should Look Out For
For many people, it takes a while to get used to sleeping in a bed that isn't their own. So, imagine how a puppy must feel when it's not only changed the location, but the entire environment, including owners—doesn't that sound stressful? That's why it is essential to keep an eye out for any of these signs to determine if your new family member needs some extra care and soothing.

Body Language
A home is a dog's safe sanctuary and moving to a new home might be causing your little pup a whole lot of anxiety, especially when it's unfamiliar with you and doesn't know how safe it should be feeling around you. One of the most common signs to indicate that your puppy is feeling stressed will be through its body language. Shaking and shivering are obvious indicators of discomfort and fear, as well as tense muscles and excessive drooling. If your puppy is itching and scratching a lot, or shedding more hair than it should be, these are

all signs to help you understand that it's stressed.

Position of ears
While it might be difficult to notice since you're unfamiliar with the normal position of your new puppy's ears, most dogs tend to either perk up their ears when they're in a stressful situation or pull their ears back against their heads.

Eyes
Dogs' eyes, just like humans', can reveal a lot about how they're feeling. When a puppy is feeling stressed or facing a frightening situation, it usually gives you the side-eye with a white crescent shape appearing around its eyes. This half-moon eye is a common sign that your poor puppy is freaking out and is in need of soothing.

Barking
While it is normal for dogs to bark, barking for no reason can be a strong indication of stress—especially when they not only bark, but also resort to whimpering, whining, growling and excessive panting. This can be due to separation anxiety from its mother or previous owner, or signs of stress that will occur until it feels more comfortable and safer around you.

Destroying house equipment
Because your puppy is unfamiliar with the surroundings, it could resort to destroying furniture, doors, or anything it can get its hands on—or paws in this case. While it is a normal reaction to get mad, it is important to understand that this is only due to the stress of being in an unfamiliar environment and will need time to settle in.

There are many signs that your puppy is feeling stressed, but it is important to understand that this is not only common, but also very valid for it to feel this way. This is the time when the puppy needs to feel that it is part of a new family that will support it and smother it with love. It is best to keep your puppy close, pet it if possible, give it food and water to show that you care, while trying to establish a connection to make the stress and anxiety go away.

Taking care of a puppy isn't always an easy task, but as long as you're prepared, invested and keeping an eye out for what your newest family member needs, you'll be doing a great job. Sure, giving your buddy the best dog food you can afford is very important, but at the end of the day, dog ownership entails much more than providing food, water, and shelter. Remember that from the moment your puppy walks through the door, your home will be its home, too. Ensuring that it's a happy one will take some time and effort, but it will definitely be worth it.

Chapter 3: Training Your Puppy

Training is very important in a dog's life. It creates a stronger bond between the puppy and the owner, and plays into the dog's quality of life by providing it with the necessary mental stimulation. It helps the dog establish right from wrong using rewards for good behavior, and correction for bad behavior. Dogs need these valuable lessons to feel stable, secure, confident and happy. Training should not involve hurtful behavior, and correction should never involve any form of abuse. It's imperative that you never use shaming tactics if your dog isn't quite getting the hang of it yet; it will take time and getting frustrated won't help. Training is about encouraging your dog to behave in ways that are acceptable in your home and in public places.

Basic training
You can begin basic training with your puppy from two to four months old. Start with simple commands such as "sit" before you give it a meal. Be patient with your dog, and reward its compliance with treats. Gradually move on to "come" and "stay." Don't spend more than ten

minutes a day on tricks, and don't confuse it by teaching five commands at once.

Will you need to hire a trainer?
Hiring a trainer is advised for first-time dog owners as the amount of training information out there can be overwhelming. However, even if you have plenty of experience raising canine companions, you can always enhance your capabilities with training experts. Obedience schools are highly recommended as they not only teach your dog basic to advanced training, but they also improve your dog's social skills—which is of great importance—as well as provide you with the tools to continue its progress.

How will you know which trainer is right for you?
Ask questions. Find out what the trainer's philosophy is based on what methods they use. It's best to opt for training schools that use positive reinforcement for appropriate behavior, teaching alternative behaviors to put in place of inappropriate ones. It's vital you feel comfortable with them, and trust them with your pet.

What to expect
Change takes time as dogs learn through repetition and pick up commands gradually. Like children, your pup will go through a challenging phase as it tests its boundaries. Do not become frustrated; this is normal and as long as you remain calm and keep training as a short and fun experience, they'll hop back on board.

Training should always be fun and include lots of praise. Your dog should grow familiar with the phrase "good girl/boy" and understand that it's encouragement. This way, it will be happier, and your bond will be stronger when it's given clear boundaries.

Getting Your Puppy's Focus
At one point or another, you must face the challenge of training your dog. This can be rather tough at the beginning, but the more you practice, the better and easier it gets. One rule of thumb, though, is to grab your pup's attention and keep it focused. There are many simple and fun exercises to do help you do just that, and here are some of them.

The eye contact exercise
Eye contact is one of the most important things that your puppy needs to learn. It teaches your little pooch how to sit quietly, completely dedicating its attention to you. All you have to do is get some treats and sit beside your puppy. When your presence grabs its attention, reward it with some treats. Be patient as you try out this exercise and repeat it more than once to make sure that your puppy becomes aware of the connection.

The hand targeting exercise
Hand targeting training is known to be one of the empowering exercises for your dog. It is very simple to do. All you have to do is place the palm of your hand in front of your puppy's nose. Once your little pup touches your hand, reward it with some treats and repeat it over and over again. This exercise mainly helps your puppy stay focused and neglect any other distractions that might be around.

The impulse control exercise
This exercise is more or less a concept that has many variations for you and your puppy to work

with. You typically start this after you make sure that your puppy is well-trained in maintaining eye contact. To teach your puppy impulse control, try dropping something from the table to the floor. If your pup rushes to get it, cover it with your foot as your dog approaches. If it patiently sits and waits, reward your pup with its own treats. If it tries to reach the food, place your foot back on the food and repeat.

The distraction exercise
Distraction is what mainly affects your pup's focus and attention. For this kind of exercise, you will be needing two things: a quiet place to practice, and a clicker or a toy that your pet responds to.
Once you're all set, you can start teaching your dog how to focus on something specific by using the sound of the clicker or its favorite toy. Either of those items will grab its attention and help it focus. After you've practiced for a while, you can start to gradually increase the amount of distractions around for better results.

Being patient is an essential aspect of training your pup. Not all of us are training experts indeed. However, the more you work on these exercises with your pup, the sooner it will learn to pay attention to its training sessions.

Teaching Your Puppy Its Name

This may sound simple enough; all you have to do is give your puppy a name, use it frequently, and that's it. Sooner or later your pup will get used to it, right? While this may be true, there's more you can do to teach your puppy its name in a way that allows you to use it as a tool to potentially keep it safe.

By calling your dog's name when it's about to wander into danger, you can prevent many potential disasters, but only if the dog actually turns back to you every time. With this in mind, let's take a look at how to teach your puppy its name in a more structured way.

Get your puppy's attention

Start this process when you're at home with no distractions around and a supply of treats to use a reward. Make sure that you already have your dog's attention before you start, and avoid training if your dog is tired, overexcited, or distracted. Call your dog's name in a warm, cheerful tone and instantly reward it with a treat when it looks at you.

In most cases, your puppy will look at you just to see what's going on, but the incentive of getting a treat will allow it to associate its name with something pleasant and motivate it to look again the next time you call its name.

Now, let your puppy's attention wander and then call its name once more. As soon as it looks at you, reward it again with a treat. Repeat these steps for a maximum of 10 times in a single session and keep the training brief. If you overdo it, your puppy will get bored and lose interest, rendering the entire process useless.

Change the training location
Start mixing up the places where you have your training sessions, but stay indoors. Choose places with minimal distractions because you're still early on in the training process and you need to set your puppy up to win. Repeat the previous steps around your home and backyard in many sessions throughout the day until you can effectively get your puppy's attention every time.

Increase the time you require its attention
Now, you should try to increase the time you require its attention before rewarding it. Call

your puppy's name and when it gives you its attention, praise it immediately, but wait for a couple of seconds before giving it the treat. This way, you teach it to give you its attention for longer. Gradually increase the time until you can eventually hold your puppy's undivided attention for at least five seconds each time you call it.

Introduce distractions
Once you can reliably count on holding your puppy's attention for at least five seconds in a controlled environment, increase the difficulty level of the training by introducing some distractions. Have someone else be present in the room, give the dog a toy, or maybe even turn the TV on. Wait until it's fully distracted, then call its name. Because this is harder than the previous exercises, reward your pup immediately when it looks at you instead of waiting for five seconds.

Move it outside
Now that you can get your puppy's attention indoors even when distracted, it's time to take it up a notch and move your training outside. Start somewhere quiet and go back to the simple exercises that require a limited attention span,

then gradually work your way towards the harder exercises.

This may seem like a lot of work just to teach your puppy its name, but that's only because you're going to use it as an effective tool in numerous situations. Whether it's for getting your puppy's attention in any situation, ensuring its safety, or training it more effectively, these tips can help you successfully achieve all that with the least effort possible.

What Is a Clicker Word and Why Is It Important?

There are a lot of things that you need to learn as a new dog owner, and a lot of training to do. Every dog owner knows that they need to start training their puppies as early as possible. People start with simple things like teaching their dog its name, until it gradually reaches a comfortable level where it can recognize the clicker signal.

What is a clicker word?

The clicker itself is a relatively small gadget that is used to communicate with your puppy. This gadget has a small button that releases a noise when clicked on and lets your dog know that it will be getting a treat for a job well done. However, you don't necessarily have to use that gadget. You can use a clicker word of your choosing; it can be anything you want. It can also be a distinct sound like a clap or a whistle. If your dog is deaf, you can communicate by using light. The important thing is to have a clicker word or a sign, whatever it may be.

Shaping the dog's behavior

Puppies need to be immediately trained once they are in your house, and this is where the clicker word comes into play. One of the first things you will be teaching your dog is potty training. The clicker word will be helping you with this. You will need to take notice of your dog's behavior, and reward it every time it does its business outside instead of inside. You say the clicker word once it is done and then give it a treat. You can practice this technique with everything else that you want your dog to do.

Communication

Unfortunately, humans and dogs don't have a universal language they can use to communicate. This is exactly why your pup needs to learn a few things, starting with its name. Let's say you want to call out to your dog because it's lunchtime; how can you do that without using its name? The clicker helps you with that, too. Start by grabbing the dog's attention, call out its name, and when it responds, say the clicker word and then give it a treat. Do this repetitively, until you call out for it and it comes to you right away. This way, your dog associates its name with a treat and knows that it did a good job by responding, because you said the clicker word.

You might have noticed that the clicker word and treats go hand-in-hand. But that is only in the beginning. You need to establish that the clicker word means "you did a good job." So, you will only be using the treats at the beginning while the dog is still young. Later on, you will find yourself using the clicker word without having to hand out treats. Dogs are intelligent beings, so don't worry; the learning process won't take long.

Teaching Your Dog to Recognize and Listen to Your Voice

Getting your puppy to listen to you and follow your commands is no easy task, and it only comes from a place of trust and affection. That is why this is the best place to start once you get your new fur baby. After years of trial and error, people have found some basic rules to govern your dog's behaviors and make it follow your instructions, be they sounds, gestures, or even a look.

First and foremost, be the boss
Dogs respect authority. Show your pup who is the leader from day one. Start by always walking one step ahead and standing over it when giving a command. Make sure it understands that you will not tolerate unaccepted behavior. Using a firm tone of voice—this is not the same as a *mean* one, and definitely not shouting—when giving commands will lay down the ground rules about who is to be followed in this relationship.

Lead by encouragement
Reward your dog to lure it into listening to you. You can start by offering treats every time it follows an order. If it responds to its name, make sure you convey that this is the desired behavior and reward it even with just a pat on the back and an encouraging "good boy." Once you notice that your dog has learned this trick and it's no longer new to it, move on and save the treats for the next lesson. Refrain from provoking your pet into submission by angry demeanor, as this will only make it mistrust you and have a negative impact on your relationship.

Consistency is key
Just like humans, being sent mixed messages confuses dogs. Common words and actions are to be used with all members of the family and any other person to deal with your puppy. Actions like "sit," "stay" or "roll" need to be unified with the exact same wording at all times.

Make time for training
Dedicate a part of your daily routine for puppy training. Think of it as your quality time with your pet. Go for walks or play a few minutes of fetch before starting your session. This way, your pup can get past its excitement and release stored energy to have a somewhat clear mind and focus on your training. Experts recommend training in 15-minute sessions every day, repeating each command 5-15 times before moving on to the next one.

Affirm your commands visually
Assigning an action to each voice order makes the learning process easier for dogs. Demanding your dog to sit can be accompanied by moving the palm of your hand facing downwards in repetition. This way, your dog will be tuned to

both your voice and body gestures. This approach is specifically helpful for dogs with hearing issues, or senior ones.

Practice in different setups
Puppies can behave perfectly at home, then get totally distracted when it's playtime in the park. If you keep practicing in different environments, your dog will understand that regardless of where you are, a command is a command and has to be followed. As long as it is a secure space, show your dog that you expect obedience everywhere.

Consider professional advice
Seek guidance from experts to assist with behavior modification and help your dog learn faster. You can receive advice on how to best go about the training. However, remember to ask for references from other dog parents beforehand. You can also watch videos and attend workshops designed to suit your specific needs.

Do not give up
Keep repeating your practices over and over again. The time it takes to complete the training of laying command varies from one dog to the

other. Study the characteristics of your pup's breed and do the necessary research to manage your expectations and avoid being frustrated; otherwise, you would be setting up your dog for failure as it picks up on your energy and vibe.

Dogs are indeed man's best friends, and they'll surely do their best to please their owners once they get the hang of things. It might take your dog some time to understand what you're really asking, but be patient and try to take this process one step at a time. Once you both get used to each other and form a certain understanding, the love and happiness it brings into your life will definitely be worth the effort you put into its training.

Basic Commands All Puppies Should Learn

It is definitely fun to watch a dog roll over and play dead on command, but let's admit it; these are a bit too advanced for your new puppy to perform just yet. Training has a certain structure and logic to it, and it makes yours—and your dog's—life easier if you stick to baby steps. There are certain commands that are easier to grasp than others for most puppies, and they can come in really handy in everyday life, even contributing to your fur baby's safety and security in some situations. Here are some basic commands that every puppy should learn in the early stages of the training process.

Sit
You'll find that most experts agree that the "sit" command is the easiest for puppies to learn, and it's also one of the most important ones. This is why it is usually the first one they're taught. It teaches them discipline, and based on that, they start responding to basic training. To teach your pup the "sit" command, you need to be gentle and positive, rewarding it with treats and praise whenever it gets it right. You simply need to hold a treat in your hand, and then put it close to your dog's nose so it would recognize what it is. It would most likely try to reach up and get it, which is when you should gently guide it down with your other hand while saying "sit." When it follows your command, pet it and give it the treat. You can also make use of mealtimes by holding the food bowl up in your hand and waiting for your dog to sit naturally by itself, then rewarding it with the food once it does. Keep repeating these techniques until your puppy instinctively responds to the command upon hearing it once.

Some dogs don't respond well to being touched or manually handled during training. In that case, you can hold a treat in your hand above your dog's head while it is standing in front of a wall or an object, and move your hand toward its back while saying "sit." It will most likely sit by itself to be able to focus on the treat without being able to move back. When it does, say the clicker word and give the treat.

Down

This is a similar command to "sit" and it's particularly useful with larger dogs, since it makes them lie down in a comfortable position. When they get used to lying down on command, it becomes easier to take them out to parks and restaurants, because they'd be relaxing on the floor without you having to worry about them all the time. You can teach your dog this simple command quite easily like the previous one, but you'll put the treat a bit further down to the ground this time and somewhat closer to you. You'll find that the dog is following you down and stretching forward toward the treat. Keep saying the command, and when its belly touches the ground, say the clicker word and give it the treat. Repeat every day until it has it memorized.

If your dog tends to follow the treat without touching the ground, you can limit its space by using your own legs. Sit down on the floor with your back leaning against a wall and bend your knees to form a kind of 'tunnel' with your legs. Make your dog follow the treat in your hand, holding it on the other side of your legs. While trying to reach the treat, it will probably have to go under your bent legs, being forced to crawl on the floor. Once it reaches this position and touches the floor with its entire body, say the clicker word and reward your dog.

Heel
The "heel" command is one of the most important ones out there, because it teaches your puppy to walk next to you rather than trail back or try to outrun you. It teaches dogs discipline and how to walk next to their owners without causing any problems. It also helps them to get used to being walked on a leash. This one might be a bit trickier to teach, but with some practice, your pooch will get there. You can use a squeaky toy for this one, and you start by putting a collar and a leash on the puppy. Then you order it to sit down, and ask it to follow from that position with the squeaky toy in your hand

as you start moving forward. As you walk, repeat the command "heel," and if the puppy gets distracted, use the toy to make it focus. If it tries to outrun you, pause and give it the toy and praise it for pausing with you. After it's more focused, try repeating again until it can follow up with you without lagging behind or trying to outrun you.

Come
A lot of people consider the "come" command to be the most important of them all, because it might just end up saving your life or that of your dog one day. Puppies need to be taught this one early on, and you have to be diligent with it, as they need to really know how to follow this command. It might happen one day that your dog escapes its leash or runs toward a potential danger. This command can save it from being hit by a car or approaching strangers. So, it has to be able to immediately run back to you once it hears the word. You should never scold your dog if it fails to do so when called, and be very patient—it might get the wrong message and actually avoid you if this results in trauma. Use its favorite toy or treat to lure it while repeating the command, and be very generous with praise when it does come toward you. It's a fairly

simple order to teach, but it may take some time until your puppy can get used to it, and you shouldn't rush it at all.

Leave it / don't touch
Dogs are curious creatures by nature, and that curiosity can get them in trouble quite often. This is where the "leave it" command comes in; it can protect them from approaching a potentially dangerous object. It also helps around the house if your puppy is playing with something it should stay away from. This command is a bit complicated to teach puppies, so you need to be patient with this one as well. You can approach it by holding treats in both hands, and when the pup tries to approach one, repeat the command "leave it." When it does, give it the treat in the other hand, and praise it. That way, your dog will start getting used to the idea that some things are off-limits, and as long as you keep repeating the phrase and rewarding it, it'll be quite responsive when you order it to leave something.

The important thing is to be patient and positive with all these commands. Puppies need constant motivation and pampering to be able to respond to training, and they do deserve to get pampered. So, take your time while teaching them new things, and bring a lot of toys and treats! Nothing puts a puppy in the mood to cooperate like treats and being called a good doggie.

How to Housebreak Your Puppy
Housebreaking is crucial for a happy relationship between a pet owner and their puppy. In order to potty train your pup, you'll have to learn a few things yourself. Below are a few tried-and-tested training tips that will help you successfully house-train your puppy.

When should you start?
One of the most important steps you need to take for a happy life with your puppy is teaching it to relieve itself at the right time and place. Dog experts recommend that you start potty training your puppy when it's around three months old because by that age it will have enough bladder and bowel control to learn to hold it.

How long does it take?
It typically takes four to six months for a puppy to be fully potty trained, however, the duration can vary considerably from one pup to another; some may be fast learners while others can take

up to a year. This depends on many factors including the dog's age, personality, previous living conditions, and breed. For instance, smaller dogs such as pugs and chihuahuas have smaller bladders and higher metabolisms, which means that they have to go more often. And the more your pup has to go, the more you have to train it.

Basic housebreaking foundations
Besides the frequent walks outside, there are two main approaches to potty training your puppy; crate training and paper training. Each method has its pros and cons but they can all work if you follow the basic rules of housebreaking. Regardless of the training approach you choose, experts recommend confining the puppy to a specific space or room until it learns to do its business in the right place. Then, you can gradually give it more freedom to roam about the house.

Routine
If you fail to be consistent, your puppy will fail, too. So, be sure to keep a consistent schedule for your pup. This includes its trips outside, feeding times, and exercise routines. Stick to a regular feeding schedule for your doggie and take away

its food between meals; this way, you can regulate the times when it'll need to relieve itself. When taking your pup outside, bring it to the same spot each time because its scent will prompt it to do its business there.

Encouragement

If your puppy gets it right, reward it with treats, praise, or affection to reinforce its good behavior. But if it does something wrong, make it clear that you're not happy with it by ignoring it or firmly saying "no." Whatever you do, don't hit your pup, because this teaches it to fear you rather than love you, and this will not make it learn any faster. In fact, it will likely prolong the entire training process.

Correction

If you catch your dog in the act, say "no" in a sharp tone or clap loudly so it would know that it's doing something wrong. When it stops, take it to its designated spot to finish its business, and then praise it or give it a small treat when it's done. Thoroughly clean up accidents with a strong, dog-friendly cleanser to remove the odors that might attract your puppy back to the same spot.

Timing
Watch out for the signs telling you that your puppy needs to go potty. Whining, sniffing, circling, barking, or scratching at the door are all obvious signs that your dog needs to go. As a general rule, you should go for a bathroom run first thing in the morning and last thing at night. Also, always take your pup out after it eats, drinks, finishes an indoor playing session, or wakes up from a nap. With very young puppies, you might need to take them out every 30-60 minutes.

Crate training
Many dog owners cringe at the idea of confining their little puppies in a crate. However,
a crate will allow you to spot the signs when your puppy needs to go, making it easy to train your dog to hold it until you open the crate and let it out. Make sure that the crate is large enough for your dog to stand up, lie down, and turn around, but not so large that they can use one of the corners as a bathroom.

Don't take too long to let your puppy out, otherwise, it'll lose control and might even get the idea that it's okay to soil its living space. If this happens, it will likely think that it's okay to soil *your* living space, too. If you're using the crate for more than two hours straight, attach a dispenser to the crane to ensure that it has access to clean water.

Paper training
Paper training is perhaps the most convenient housebreaking method for busy dog owners but this option comes with one tricky complication. Ideally, your pup would learn to hold it indoors and only do its business outdoors. Paper and puppy pads reinforce the two opposing sides at the same time, which can be confusing for your puppy if you decide to take it outside later when it grows up. However, if you're incapable of taking your dog out several times a day, paper training can be a suitable alternative, as long as it gets used to an approved spot at home.

House soiling is one of the main reasons why many dogs end up in shelters or on the streets. Very few pet owners are willing to put up with a dog that destroys their rugs and flooring, or leaves a foul mess for them to clean after a long, tiring day. This is why it's important to start potty training your puppy early on to prevent bad habits from forming and becoming harder to control in the future. Don't worry if there are setbacks; housebreaking requires consistency, persistence, and patience. As long as you keep at it, your puppy will eventually learn.

How to Crate Train Your Puppy

Crates are commonly used for transporting dogs from one place to another, but they can do a lot more than that. By offering a private, enclosed space, a crate takes advantage of a dog's natural instincts to be a den animal, providing it with a secure canine lair where it can be comfortable.

Not only will your puppy be safe in its crate but your sanity and peace of mind will also be preserved when you can rest assured that your puppy isn't chewing up your furniture or soiling your house while you're out. However, your puppy isn't likely to get used to the idea of a crate right away. To make crate training a little easier for you, we've assembled the best tips from the dedicated dog experts.

Choose the right crate

Before you get started on crate training, you must first know how to choose the best one for your pup. The very concept behind why crates are used for housebreaking is because dogs are very clean creatures by nature and they don't like a urine-soaked living space any more than you do. This is also why the size of the crate matters the most. Find a well-ventilated crate that's just big enough for your puppy to stand up, lie down, and turn around comfortably.

If the crate is too large, your dog may think that it's okay to use one of the corners as a bathroom and sit comfortably away from the mess, which can encourage future accidents around the house. And if it's too small, your dog will not enjoy staying in it and this will likely make potty training a lot harder for you in return.

Remember that the crate has to accommodate your puppy as it grows, so choose one that's appropriate for the expected full-grown size of your dog and use a divider to accommodate your pup's smaller size for the time being. Alternatively, you can purchase a crate that comes with an adjustable partition that you can adapt to the size of your puppy as it grows.

Get your puppy to love the crate
For a successful training process, the crate should always be associated with something pleasant. Make the crate more inviting by lining it with blankets and putting a few toys inside. Place the crate in a high-activity area such as the living room, where you and the other household members spend a lot of time. When you first introduce your pup to the crate, encourage it to enter by going down to its level and speaking to it in a happy voice. You can also lure it in by dropping a few teats near the crate, then leave some just inside the door, and finally, toss a few all the way inside. If it still refuses to go in at first, that's alright, don't force it to enter. Whether it takes a few minutes or a few days, keep tempting it with treats until it willingly walks inside.

Gradually condition your puppy to get used to the crate

Introduction
At first, bring your puppy to the crate for 10-minute breaks and offer it motivating treats or distracting toys when it goes inside. Once your pup is inside, sit silently near the crate for about

five minutes and then leave the room for a few minutes. When you return, sit quietly for a short while and then let your pup out of the crate. Repeat this process at least twice a day and gradually increase the duration of time you leave it in the crate.

Association

To get your puppy to associate bathroom time with crate time, take it for a walk every time it comes out of the crate. Once you reach the stage where your pup stays calmly in its crate for 30 minutes with you out of sight, you can start leaving it inside when you're gone for short time periods. Keep letting your pup in the crate for short periods every now and then when you're home so it doesn't associate crate time with abandonment.

Sleep

Once your pup is used to being alone in its crate for a couple of hours without getting anxious, you can let it sleep there at night. This can take days or weeks depending on your dog's temperament among other factors but the most important thing is to resist the temptation to rush the conditioning process. Learning takes time but if you remain patient and consistent, your puppy will eventually learn to love its crate for years to come. When crating your puppy overnight, it's usually recommended that you put the crate in your bedroom or on hallway outside your bedroom door because it will likely need to go outside during the night and you need to be able to hear it when it whines to be let out. Always make sure that your pup has access to fresh water when you're leaving it in its crate.

Never leave your puppy in its crate all day
A crate isn't a magical bypass for potty training. If it's not used properly, the crate will feel like a prison rather than a shelter for your dog and this will make it feel anxious, trapped, and abandoned. If your pup feels neglected, it will most likely act out in return. Dogs need several bathroom breaks as well as play and feeding times. Young puppies, in particular, shouldn't be kept crated for more than three or four hours at a time because they can't control their bladder and bowels long periods of time.

Crate training your puppy may take some time and effort but once you get the hang of it, it will come in handy in a variety of situations. Whether you want to limit your pup's access to the house until it learns all the house rules or you want to take it to the vet while protecting your car's precious seats, the previous tips can help make your dog's crate experience a lot more pleasant. Remember that even if your puppy's crate is its den, just as you wouldn't want to spend most of your time in a room, your dog shouldn't spend most of its time in a crate.

Chapter 4: Dealing with Behavioral Problems

Having a dog means having a life companion. People see and treat their dogs as if they are their own kids. That is why, just like you prepare for having a baby by reading tons of books about parenting and how to raise a child, learning how to care for a dog should be as important, if not more, given the fact that you are of two different species after all.

Not so long ago, psychology did not play too big a role in canine health and care, but the times have changed. Nowadays, raising a pup requires a deep understanding of your dog's mental and emotional state, and this is how you'll identify, work on and solve most of the common behavioral issues. Let's take a look at some of them.

Being on Furniture

Almost every pet owner allows their dog to access their furniture and be comfortable with them on the couch, all cuddled up. But if your dog is particularly destructive, gnawing away furniture corners, or is too tiny to safely climb on your couch, it is better to keep your furry friend off your furniture. But once it gets used to the luxury, snatching away your favorite couch spot, it is difficult to get it off. Also, if it is not potty trained yet, you might have to get your hands on some baby wipes and detergents to wash off the stains and the odor.

So, what can you do to keep your dog from hopping on furniture? Here are a few tips to try out.

Use commands "off" or "down"
Training your dog to follow instructions and commands is crucial and can be particularly helpful for this behavioral problem. The "off" command is used to get your puppy off the furniture, and the "down" command is used to get it to lie down on the floor. Gently lift your dog and say "off" while putting it down, followed by offering a treat. Keep on doing this until your dog follows the pattern and realizes that it is better to keep off the furniture at all times. Command training can also make your dog more obedient, calm and confident.

Say "place"
If you've designated a comfortable place for your dog, it has no reason to be on furniture. A cozy bed with soft cushions accompanied by its

favorite toys and enough room to roll over sounds like an ideal dog space. When you see your dog climbing over furniture, say "place" in a commanding tone. Train it to go to its place thereafter. It can be done by showing it the way step by step, and offering a reward every time it follows. You can also leave several treats on its bed. At first, it's a good idea to keep the bed near the couch to give it a sense of familiarity.

Use a crate
When you aren't home, use a crate to isolate your dog from certain areas, especially your main living space. Make the crate extremely comfortable for your dog so that it does not feel the desire to break the boundaries. This is helpful when you are not at home, since it might make it easier to keep the house cleaner. You can also use a spare room for your dog with little to no furniture while you are out.

Block access to furniture
A tactic that you can use in the early days of training your dog to keep off furniture is to block access to it by placing a few chairs upside down on the furniture, or other lighter blockages. A small table or chair on the couch will leave no

room for your dog to jump on. You can now buy products designed for this purpose, as well. Your dog will eventually give up.

Your pup being on furniture is not a big deal, but it is surely better to avoid damages and repairs, which is why training is important. Once you have a well-behaved puppy, it's pretty easy to lay down some rules and set limits. If you don't want to go for physical barriers or spend time on teaching certain commands, especially at first, you can spray special products on areas you want your puppy to stay away from—they contain harmless and safe components, but give off unpleasant smells that will discourage your dog to explore these items and places.

Bolting and Running Away

Have you ever witnessed your dog bolting and running away as soon as you open the front door? It may seem like a fun sight to watch in the beginning, but you will get anxious the next moment. Running away can be dangerous for your dog as it can get lost or might not notice a moving car. Especially if it does not respond to the "come" command, it will be difficult to take it out for safe walks or provide it with the sufficient amount of exercise.

This behavior usually occurs in your pup due to loneliness, boredom or simply getting the sense of being abandoned in an enclosed space. Dogs need large spaces to sense freedom and thus will take advantage of the slightest opportunity given to them. Other factors that can cause your dog to bolt are lack of socialization, seeing other dogs around or lack of obedience training. So, you need to up your game and train your dog to be calmer and control impulsive behavior.

Obedience training
Training your dog to sit, lie down or eat according to instructions is every dog owner's desire, as it shows control and obedience on the dog's part. Start to train your puppy in its younger weeks to embed this compliant behavior for the rest of its life. Simple ways to obedience train are providing rewards or treats upon compliance, not encouraging any unacceptable behavior, and being patient. Once trained, your dog would be able to follow instructions smoothly even off-leash, eventually preventing it from ever running away.

Recall training
The purpose of recall training is to make sure your dog responds to the cue when you call out

to it, even when it's running off in excitement. It probably won't return on the first call, but if it does, reward it with a treat. This will become a habit and thus it will always respond to your calls in the future. With efficient and consistent training, it should gradually stop running away in the first place.

But do not be all content yet, as your dog is returning only to receive its treat. Recall training can take time, but once your dog starts coming back on call without the use of treats, that's when you have truly succeeded.

Taking your dog out more often
One of the reasons that your dog would run away is to experience freedom and socialize with others. If it is not encountering enough 'outside' experiences, it is bound to bolt from your house. Take a walk in a park or play with your dog in the yard as much as you can. Throwing balls, fetching toys or playing with Frisbees can create a bond between the two of you. So, the next time you open the door, your pup would want you by its side instead of it running away to play with others.

If you own a house with a yard, try to border it with fences so that your dog cannot get out of the premises. In the end, these are natural dog instincts and combating them can prove to be arduous. Instead, you can simply make a good plan and follow it with consistency.

Destructive Chewing
Everyone who owns a puppy knows the pain of losing valuable objects just because the pooch destroys it. Chewing can occur due to a rise in curiosity, being anxious or simply because it is bored. If not stopped at an early stage, it will become difficult to control your dog when it grows up. Even if your puppy has been teething, it is necessary to control this behavior of destructive chewing.

Get some chew toys
You can easily find various kinds of chew toys that are safe for your dog. Once you see it getting hold of an object, immediately distract it with a chew toy. While buying the toys, you need to consider the material and quality, as well as the size and strength of your pup. If your dog seems to easily destroy the toy, you have to make sure that it does not swallow or choke on the ripped parts. Buy safer and sturdier toys for avid chewers to prevent hazards.

Take your dog out to exercise
All puppies need some level of exercise to ensure healthy growth. Exercise will not only maintain the mental and physical well-being of your dog but will also drain its excess energy. Exercise also releases endorphins, known as happy hormones, which will calm your pup down afterward, making it less likely to try and find objects to chew on. Once it has spent all the extra energy, you will have less of a hard time controlling it.

Use deterrent sprays
This tactic works both for destructive chewing and mouthy behavior in your dog. Using a deterrent spray with an unpleasant taste on objects that your dog tends to chew will make it stop eventually. If done regularly, it will realize the unappealing bitterness it tastes every time and will avoid reaching it in the first place.

Puppy proofing
Similar to baby proofing, getting your house ready for your puppy can save your valuable objects from being damaged. It will also save your pup from potential hazards. Loose wires should be securely coiled or covered; medicines and chemicals should be inaccessible to your

dog; books, shoes and other chewable items should be kept in boxes or on higher shelves, completely out of reach. Objects that are extremely important should be kept in a closed room. Your dog may simply lose interest if it doesn't find any curious objects lying around.

Supervising your dog in its early days can result in a better attitude as it grows up. You should not let it get away with destructive behavior because that will only encourage it to continue. Instead, practice time-out sessions by ignoring and not interacting with it. Crate training can also help protect your house until your puppy is fully trained.

Excessive Barking and Whining

Dogs are big attention seekers, especially when they are pampered a lot. But attention-seeking behavior can also be a sign of pain or agitation. At times, your dog can be barking non-stop, annoying you and your neighbors. This situation can be difficult to decipher but it is possible that your dog is suffering from some medical issues or anxiety problems. To deal with whining and barking, you first need to figure out the underlying cause of this behavioral problem.

Some overlooked factors are lack of attention by owners or being left alone for a long time, separation anxiety, and inadequate social interaction, change of environment or feeling sick.

As a dog owner, you shouldn't encourage the whining behavior by looking at, petting or picking up your dog. It will only stimulate its whining as it will get used to this pampering pattern. Also, do not enforce too much negative behavior toward it, especially when you are working for longer hours and it is left alone at home. Instead, try to keep your emotions balanced as it will help your puppy to behave.
So, what exactly can be done to prevent this behavior?

Analyze the issue
If you hear your dog whining or barking in several pitches or weird noises over time, you might want to decode what it wants to say. Often, it can indicate different things, some of which could be serious like when your dog is in pain or is feeling sick. If you pay attention to its whining, you can understand the different sounds it makes and simply ignore it when it only seems to seek attention. Knowing the root

cause can give you a good direction for the treatment.

Provide more exercise
Taking your dog out to exercise can improve almost any behavioral problem, which is also true for its excessive barking and whining. Exercising can make your dog get tired sooner than usual, and once it is tired, there will be no energy left in it to whine or bark. Playing with it or walking it in the park can also give you both some quality time, which could ultimately alleviate the problem.

Act normal
Your dog might get nervous when you leave the house and overexcited when you return. And when you are around, it whines for attention. You need to act neutral and not show any emotions when you come and go, at least for a while, to help it learn. Not paying attention and ignoring can lessen the whining and barking. Enact a little skit of coming and going for a few minutes at regular intervals with your keys, shoes, and jacket. This will make it get used to your leaving without making a big deal out of it.

If you feel that the whining issue is not behavioral, you should take your dog to a veterinarian, as there could be a serious underlying health problem. You can also hire a certified trainer to assess and address this issue successfully.

Mounting

Although mounting is a common behavioral problem witnessed in growing dogs, it can get annoying and embarrassing at times. Dogs prefer to hump a stuffed toy, a human leg or other dogs. There are several causes of this, the most common being sexual instincts related to reproduction. However, you can also find neutered dogs humping around, which can be due to stress, anxiety or out of habit. At times, dogs hump to show dominance over other canines. Your dog might also hump to grab your attention to play with it.

Whatever the cause is, treating this behavioral problem in your dog can save you and your dog from embarrassment when other people are around. Even though it is a completely normal act in dogs, seeing it frequently could indicate an underlying problem and thus needs to be prevented.

Drain excess energy
Exercising your dog can treat a number of behavioral problems, humping being one of them. When you take it out to exercise or for long runs, it will get rid of some excess energy and will likely feel too tired to mount. Humping requires a lot of energy, and an exhausted dog will simply not bother with it.

Ignore the behavior
If you have observed your dog's mounting pattern and figured that it is doing it to grab your attention, you need to start ignoring its actions, especially when it targets your leg. Face away or walk away to another room. If done frequently, your dog will realize that it will not gain attention by doing this, and you do not encourage this behavior. This way, it will eventually stop performing this action.

Distract your puppy
As soon as you see your dog mounting, distract it by picking up its favorite toy or a treat and wait until you get its attention. As soon as it looks, take some time to go to another room for it to discontinue the mounting action. Then, reward

it with a toy. This will interrupt the humping action and it will start playing instead. Be sure to wait until you offer it the reward or the toy, otherwise, it would only serve as another mounting object for your dog. If you fail to grab its attention while it's mounting, drop something—preferably its favorite toy—that would make enough noise to distract and redirect it.

Say "no" and practice time-outs
Use strict commands to control your dog's humping actions. Saying "no" sternly can startle it and make it realize that its actions are not appreciated. Do not lash out or show anger; try to be strict but composed. If it doesn't listen, gently lift it and take it to another room for a little time-out. Ensure that there are no toys or objects in the room to mount on. Once it has been alone for a few minutes, its mounting behavior should have subsided temporarily. Following this repeatedly can help solve this problem.

If none of the tricks work and you feel that the mounting behavior in your dog is a health problem, then immediately seek medical help. A vet can figure out the cause, which will make it easier to treat it.

Mouthing

We've already established that, as a dog owner, you need to look out for several factors that might go unnoticed. One such factor is mouthiness in dogs. Mouthing is when a dog uses its mouth to nibble, play with, or "herd" people or other animals. It is often a sign of affection, but can get serious or destructive over time. A few precautions should be taken if you notice excessive mouthing in your dog.

Get chew toys or bones

Puppies who are about six months old tend to be teething, so mouthing can be common among them. But if your dog is old enough and is still mouthing, you can get it a few chew toys or bones to gnaw on. As soon as you notice it putting its mouth over clothes or hands, throw a toy in its direction. This will teach it to alter its focus.

Let your dog exercise and socialize

This way, not only is your pup being distracted, but it is also draining its excessive energy. Playing with other dogs can make it understand its own behavior when they try to attack it during a friendly play. But if your dog is less than one year old, consider skipping the runs and long walks, as it can affect its growth and developing bones.

Teach bite inhibition

Do not make the mistake of shutting down your dog's mouth when it starts biting or nibbling on your hands. Instead, take a gentler approach. You can use three techniques to teach bite inhibition, which is when your dog will stop painful biting and become much lighter on its jaw control.

Exclaiming

You can pretend to scream in pain when your dog bites you, which will startle it and it will let go. This will make it realize over time that this unwanted activity hurts you, hopefully making it gradually stop.

Ignoring

If screaming does not work, ignore your dog afterward. This is the last thing it wants at this point, given the playful mood it is in. If you do this repeatedly, it will learn to avoid biting to continue playing with you.

Leaving
The last thing you can do is to scream and leave the spot. Move somewhere it cannot follow you and is restricted to enter. Do not show up for about 20 minutes. Practicing this method of time-out will cause separation anxiety and will teach your dog to follow the pattern next time.

Use a spray deterrent
This is another tactic you can try to keep your dog away from the specific parts it tends to bite periodically. A bad tasting spray, if applied on those parts of your body and clothes, will repel your dog from biting or nibbling on them. Continue this for about 10 days and you will see it backing off, eventually reducing its mouthing habit.

Some dog breeds are more prone to mouthing and herding, as it's coded in their instincts. Try to differentiate between playful nibbling and aggressive biting—those are two very different behaviors. In any case, it is important that you be patient with your dog, as preventing mouthing behavior can take time. But upon practicing these tips consistently, it should fetch results.

Pulling on the Leash
Have you ever had trouble with your dog constantly pulling on the leash while you are out on a walk? Well, you are not alone. Leash pulling occurs when your dog is excited and wants to move faster than you. It gets a bit difficult to catch up with the speed of your dog as it naturally possesses a faster pace than humans.

It is necessary to train your pup to retain leash manners as it can get stressful for you. It could also lead to your dog to tug hard and let loose, which is the last thing you want.

By training your dog to prevent excessive leash pulling, you will have the comfort of walking at a sustained pace, while your dog will pause along with you or wait for your permission to relieve itself at a particular spot.

You could use a few effective tips and tricks for this training, which will help you keep your puppy under total control while on a leash.

Get the right accessories
Uninformed dog owners would simply buy a leash without knowing the types out there, and the effect it would have on their dogs. Get more

information on the type of collar, harness, and leash that would be suitable for your dog, according to its size and breed, or ask for help. We recommend using a regular leash and a no-pull dog harness if your puppy tends to have this problem. You might want to avoid using electronic collars or choke chains as they could cause discomfort to your dog. Use other methods to leash train instead.

Use rewards

Occasional rewards in the form of treats or a favorite toy are useful in garnering your dog's attention. Use it while you train your dog on a leash. Walking one step at a time—while holding your dog's attention using a reward—will make it magically adapt its movement to you. Show control and say "no" when it insists on moving forward by tugging at the string. Once it calms down, praise it and offer a treat. This will slowly build an instinct in it to follow your orders, especially when on a leash.

Using rewards can also work while practicing loose leash training. Introducing distractions slowly and being consistent with this training will eventually result in success.

Stand still and change direction

Even after going through multiple loose-leash training sessions, your dog would pull on the leash at times when particularly excited or filled with enthusiasm. Either get it some exercise at home before going out for a walk to subside its energy, or use tactics like standing still or changing direction when it insists on walking faster. When your dog starts pulling, be glued at the spot for a while and then turn around to walk in the opposite direction. This will make it realize that its behavior is unacceptable, and that it doesn't get what it wants by pulling.

Pulling on the leash is a behavioral problem that will take time to augment, so be patient and consistent in training. Some dogs are significantly more energetic than others, so it might be a good idea to resort to professional training if that is the case with your pup. No matter what your special case is, though, remember that you pulling harder on the leash in return will only be counterproductive, so keep a calm and assertive attitude and don't try to solve this problem with muscle strength.

Resource Guarding
If your dog hides its possessions or tries to protect them when someone tries to touch any, it

can be a sign of resource guarding. You can also spot this behavioral problem in your pooch when it starts eating faster, for fear of its food being taken away, especially when you come closer to its bowl. Resource guarding in dogs is the phenomenon when your pup becomes possessive of its belongings—or you—and shows aggression to protect them. Although it is a common problem in many canines, this behavior shouldn't be encouraged and treated at the earliest.

Your puppy may also growl or bark at strangers or fellow dogs who are near its belongings.

This behavior of resource guarding occurs in your dog due to its natural predator instincts. Dogs are supposed to 'guard' people and objects, which can reflect as a negative trait at times. But it doesn't mean that your dog is being dominant or that you have 'spoiled' it too much. You just need to implement a few changes to curb this problem.

Use the desensitization technique

This technique involves using triggers to approach your dog by slowly increasing the intensity. If you have noticed resource guarding in your dog due to the presence of another canine, introduce a furry companion to your dog and slowly lead it towards your dog's belongings. It will be intense in the beginning, but once it calms down a bit, reward it with a treat. Get its friend closer this time and follow the pattern. It will understand that the other dog means no harm and sharing can lead to rewards.

To treat this problem with your dog's food, take baby steps to approach its food bowl while it is eating. Start by standing in the corner of the room and slowly reaching the bowl. When it does not growl, offer it a treat. The journey from the corner to the food bowl can take some time, but you just need to be patient. Offering treats will make it realize that your approach toward its food bowl is pleasant and not a threat at all.

Practice "give" and "take"
Make your dog familiar with the words "give," "take" and "trade." When it comprehends the meanings and gestures, ask for any of its favorite belongings. You will have to be patient and request several times in the beginning, but once it does, offer it a treat. This give-and-take tactic can help it realize the importance of sharing.

Try changing the eating environment
At times, the environment in which your dog eats can be a trigger itself. Placing your dog's

bowl of food in an enclosed corner can make it feel isolated and unaware of the activities in its surroundings. Try moving the food bowl in different areas and inspect its changed behavior. You could also play games in that space to make it more familiar and engaging for your pup.

If you don't keep up with the training, it is possible for your dog to rebuild this issue of resource guarding. It is not something permanent or temporary, and thus needs to be addressed all the time.

<u>Separation Anxiety</u>

If you find your dog nervously wagging its tail while you are leaving your house and in total chaos when you return, it might be a sign of your dog suffering from separation anxiety. If not trained, dogs can develop this behavioral problem that could lead to self-injury or loss of multiple valuable possessions through destruction.

Separation anxiety occurs when your puppy is left alone at home for a long time or when there is a sudden change in the schedule. Other factors that might be responsible are a change of residence or the death of a family member.

Excessive chewing on objects, destruction of belongings, howling, moving in fixed patterns or redundant urination in some cases are a few symptoms of separation anxiety in dogs. If not treated sooner, it could become worse. Training for separation anxiety from your puppy's early days can be beneficial for both of you in the long run.

Get your dog comfortable
A few tricks you could pull off are leaving its favorite chew toys with it—as nibbling and gnawing will stimulate a calming effect—and leaving some of your old clothes that smell like you by its side. You could also leave the radio or TV on at a low volume, particularly soft music or white noise. It will help your dog get more relaxed and feel surrounded by a virtual presence.
If the case is worse, you can get a crate, which will restrict its entry into unwanted spaces. Making your dog's space cozy with a bed, some food, water, toys, and enough space to feel free will slowly teach it that being separated from you for longer hours is alright.
Distract your puppy with its favorite toy five minutes prior to leaving the house. This will grab its attention and prevent it from realizing your absence.

Practice short separation intervals
Training your dog for short separation intervals when you are home can work as well. Place your dog in another enclosed space where it is comfortable and show up every few minutes, working your way up to about two hours. It will initially become anxious, but eventually, it will realize that this isn't a big deal and you will always show up after a while. Practice this with your puppy multiple times, increasing the time interval during each session. Also, be sure to leave its favorite toys with it, and provide enough food and water.

Obedience training
When a dog is obedient and follows the instructions, it is in more control of its emotions and knows better. Train your dog to sit, lie down, stay, or greet the guests only after they approach it. These habits will make the dog more relaxed and respectful, which ultimately would reflect on its behavior when you leave it alone for a few hours.

Training a dog to combat separation anxiety is not easy, and may involve some heartbreak. If you think that the problem is more serious than you anticipated, take your dog to a veterinarian to get its anxiety checked and to receive the appropriate prescription.

Jumping on People

It is extremely cute to watch your puppy getting excited about seeing new people and jumping on them, but it will continue to do so when it grows into an adult, which can get ridiculous at times. Some people might not like it and so you need to train your dog in order to stop this behavior. By jumping on people, your dog is seeking attention from you and the people it sees. However, this can not only be unwelcomed by a few people, but can also be dangerous in case of the elderly and children.

Control your dog with a leash

Having your puppy on a leash all the time is not something you'd prefer, but it is necessary to exude control. When your guests arrive, put your dog on the leash and let it calm down. Once you see the excitement fading away, take the leash off and allow it to greet the new people. If it is still not calm, gently place it in an enclosed room and let it play with its favorite toy. This will drain its energy, making it behave more steadily. If this still doesn't work, put it on a leash again and allow it to greet the guests under your control.

Train and reward
Training your dog in its early years will be edifying later. The most basic thing that your dog should know is to be on all its four paws when instructed. This can be done by praising it when it is calm and on the ground. Your puppy would also learn better if you reward it with treats after it follows the instructions. When it does not follow, ignore or freeze while being stern. Make it a habit for it to calmly sit on all its four paws before eating a meal, getting a treat or receiving petting. This will train it and become a habit, eventually making it more relaxed and poised. This tactic is called counter-command, where an alternate behavior is fortified in order to naturally diminish the unwanted one.

Time-out
Before your puppy starts jumping upon seeing new people, it is better for you to train it first. As soon as you come home and it jumps on you, do not encourage this behavior. Ignore and move to another room where it cannot follow you. Reappear after five minutes and repeat. Keep on doing this until your puppy greets you with a

calmer attitude. Do not pet or play with it when you show up for the first time. You can show affection once it greets you in a composed manner, which will make it realize the importance of being calm.

You can also take the help of a friendly stranger to train your dog when you are out in the park or walking on the street. Let your puppy approach the stranger and notice its behavior. Request the person to offer it a treat, in case you happen to have one, once it obeys to sit on all four paws. If the attempt is successful, congratulations, your puppy is adapting to being calmer around strangers.

Aggression

Aggression in dogs might be the most challenging issue for the owners to deal with. Continuous barking, growling, snapping, tail wagging, lunging or biting show the signs of aggression and a very serious behavioral problem. A lot of dog owners have faced this issue and taken professional help to overcome it.

Dog aggression behavior is classified into various types. Here are the most common types:

Fearful Aggression: When the dog is scared of being cornered.

Protective Aggression: When it feels the urge to protect its house and family members.

Territorial Aggression: Even if it knows the person, the dog may growl and show aggression to any infiltrator who has entered its space.

Social Aggression: When not socialized enough, the dog would either feel secluded or superior in front of other dogs or people.

With some patience and consistency, you can deal with aggression in your dog, starting with a few simple tricks.

Decode the cause
Unless you are aware of the issue or the root cause, it is nearly impossible to treat your dog's bad behavior. Once you have figured it out, you can take the necessary steps toward an appropriate solution, making it practical enough to solve the problem. You will have to closely monitor your dog for a few days, make a note of the pattern it follows and notice the attributes

that cause the aggression. This should give you a basic idea of the problem.

Encourage socializing
Your dog's aggressive behavior could be due to a lack of socializing. You need to take your dog out for walks in dog parks or in streets with people. You could also request the help of a friend who wouldn't mind playing with your dog. Keep it on the leash when you go outside to avoid biting and jumping. Once it gets familiar with the surroundings and starts mingling with other canines, you have solved one problem of poor interaction in your dog.

Desensitization technique
This is a helpful tactic when your dog is exposed to fear-related aggression. According to the first tip, once you have figured out the cause or trigger that creates aggression in your pup, you have to use it to treat the issue. This technique is called desensitization and works most of the time. Expose the cause in front of your dog slowly and wait for its aggression to subside. Offer it a treat when it's calm. You can keep reducing the distance of the cause or trigger toward your dog and offer more treats along the way. It will take some time and lots of sessions

for your dog to be completely quiet in the presence of the cause, but it will be worth it.

If these tricks don't seem to solve the problem, consult a vet or hire a professional trainer, as aggression in dogs is the most difficult issue to treat. Do it for the sake of your dog and for the safety of others to completely eliminate any kind of threat.

Digging

If your once-enticing lawn is no longer dazzling, with brown pits and muddy texture all around, you know you have to blame your dog. Digging can occur as a natural instinct in your dog or can also be due to boredom, excitement, a tactic to preoccupy itself, or hunting. Dogs dealing with separation anxiety or simply destructive behavior tend to dig more often, resulting in dirty patches everywhere. It is not only frustrating to see your lawn being destroyed frequently, but also leaves you with the responsibility of cleaning a dirty dog every once in a while.

To solve this behavioral problem in your dog, go through these tips to incorporate them into your training.

Use unpleasant deterrents
Once you have figured out the spots that your dog loves to dig in particular, you can use a few objects to cover those up. Using rocks that are not pointy or fencing out the area can keep your dog away from digging. You can also use a few smelly deterrents that your dog would despise, such as vinegar or citrus extracts. Your dog might figure out other suitable spots to dig so you need to pay attention to its actions and switch the deterrents to that spot. This will take your dog by surprise and will eventually make it visit the lawn less than before.

Get your dog engaged in other activities
One of the main reasons for digging is boredom and lack of activity in your dog. If you are not able to spend more time with it due to a busy schedule, you need to readjust your daily calendar and take at least an hour off to play with it. This will not only be beneficial in developing your bond but will also strike out your dog's boredom. Plus, it will be a fun hour for you to relax in your busy day and de-stress. Another advantage of scheduling this hour is that it will make your dog tired due to the

exercise and playing, and so it will not be able to expend its energy in digging. It is a complete win-win situation.

Make a sandbox
It is time for you to put your creative insights to work and create a sandbox for your puppy. You can place it near its usual digging spots. You can play with the design of the sandbox by placing preferred fencing designs and heights. When you catch your pup digging elsewhere, say "no" firmly, gently grab it and direct it toward the sandbox. Once it obeys the order, treat it with a reward. Follow this pattern for a few days. You can also hide treats in the sandbox to encourage your dog to use it for digging.

If you notice your dog digging under the fence, it would mean only one thing: the desire to escape. Use higher fences and place wire meshes underneath. And to naturally stop your dog from behaving this way, use the tips we've mentioned above.

Chapter 5: Grooming Your Puppy

When you're thinking of welcoming a new puppy to your home, you shouldn't overlook the fact that grooming is a major part of dog care. Especially with certain breeds, grooming may not be a walk in the park, and some dogs will demand it more than others. You can start the process at an early stage to get your puppy used to it, making both of your lives easier in the long run.

The first that pops up in your mind might be a nice shower when we mention dog grooming—and it is surely important—but it includes other steps and routines that you can't really pick and choose from. Grooming needs to be considered as a whole, and it's an essential part of your puppy's health and well-being.

Bathing

Unlike what you see in many cute doggie videos, most dogs actually don't enjoy baths, which means that you will need to associate bath time with something pleasant and positive. You will need to provide your puppy with a lot of treats, toys, and praise before and after bathing, so it considers it a positive occasion.

When it's time for a good bath, you need to be ready with a dog-appropriate shampoo, a brush, a towel, and preferably a partner who can help you through the process. After that, you can follow our tips to make sure you have an enjoyable time cleaning your fur baby.

Location

Start by knowing where you'll be bathing your puppy. Will it be outdoors? Or in the bathtub? Once you figure this out, get your puppy used to it without water and offer treats and toys when it does. This way, it will understand that this place is for playing and treats.

After a couple of times, start adding warm water to the bathtub until you are sure that your puppy is totally comfortable with it.

Safety

Before bathing your puppy, make sure to protect its ears. If water gets into its ears, it could be very uncomfortable for your pooch and may cause health problems. You can add a cotton ball into your puppy's ears, but if you're not able to, you can just try to avoid getting any water inside.

You should also avoid getting shampoo near your puppy's eyes and mouth. To be able to do that, you should start washing from the neck down and then move on to the rest of the body. You can use a damp washcloth in order to clean the face.

Washing and drying
After thoroughly washing your puppy with shampoo and rinsing it well with lukewarm water, start drying it. If your puppy is not scared of blow dryers, you can use it on a low setting and from a distance. However, most dogs are not comfortable with the sound. In that case, you can simply use a towel and be sure to dry every part of your puppy's body.

After both of you are comfortable with it, bathing can be a good opportunity for some bonding. Treats, toys, and praise are very important to make your puppy understand that it's fun. However, bathing too often can be unhealthy for your puppy as the coat needs its natural oils to remain soft and silky. How often you should give your puppy a bath depends on each breed and how long the hair is, but bathing more than once a week can strip away all the natural oils from the skin. Leaving your puppy too long without a bath can also damage the coat, especially for long-haired breeds. The ideal time to bathe your puppy is when the coat starts collecting dirt and looking dull, or when the odor starts to get less than pleasant.

Brushing Fur

There's no doubt that grooming improves your puppy's health and makes it look clean and beautiful. But if your puppy didn't get used to the grooming process from an early stage and is not comfortable with being handled, the process could be complicated and could take a lot of time.

Some people may think that regular brushing is only necessary for long-haired breeds, but in fact, it's essential to all breeds, even short-haired ones. Brushing your puppy's fur at least every couple of days removes dead hair, which can reduce the amount of shedding. It also distributes the natural oils on your puppy's skin, which makes the hair stronger, healthier and cleaner. Regular brushing will also prevent matting, which can turn out to be an extremely uncomfortable health issue.

Desensitizing your puppy

The first thing you should do before brushing your puppy's fur is to make sure that it's comfortable with being handled, especially if it doesn't like being touched. Once you bring a new pup to the house, start by holding your hand in front of its nose, and when it starts to get near and touches your hand, praise it and give it a treat. Repeating this process several times a day for a week will make your puppy comfortable with your hands. After that, start touching the puppy from under the chin, then move on to the rest of the body. Do this gently and while providing treats. Once your puppy gets used to your hands, start touching its paws, tail, and face gently while it's calm. If it lets you do this, then it's okay with being handled, and you can move to the next step. If it starts getting aggressive or pulling itself away, then you've gone too fast and will need to slow it down.

The right equipment
Visit the pet shop—or search online—to get the right brush for your puppy's fur. Pin-head brushes may not be comfortable for short-haired dogs, so if you're willing to get one, make sure that your pup is totally okay with it, and that it doesn't hurt. For regular brushing, you can get an all-purpose brush, or as a comb. Especially if

you own a long-haired pup, you might want to invest in a detangling brush and a flea comb, as well.

Introduction and method

Before brushing, let your pup see and smell the comb as much as possible so it wouldn't be scared of it. Begin brushing its fur from the neck down. For the first few times, try to brush gently and quietly while you reward it with a lot of treats and praise.

If you feel like the process will take a lot of time, try to make it short and then increase it each time. You can start by brushing the neck, paws, and tail, and once you do that successfully, you will be able to brush the rest of its body without any hassle.

Brushing your puppy doesn't only make its hair healthier and shiny, but it also allows you to be familiar with its body and how it feels. Knowing how your puppy's skin and coat feels will enable you to notice if there's anything unusual, which can help you detect skin problems at an early stage.

Brushing Teeth

As mentioned before, grooming goes beyond brushing and bathing your puppy; it should also include brushing its teeth on a regular basis. Recent studies found that most dog owners neglect brushing their dog's teeth, and when they're two years old, dogs start showing signs of gum disease and other dental problems. If you don't take care of your puppy's teeth and any signs of dental issues, the only way to cure it is with mechanical cleaning. This option can be expensive and uncomfortable for your dog. The best way to prevent any dental problems is by regularly brushing your puppy's teeth once the adult teeth begin to grow.

Getting your dog used to toothbrushing

Before your puppy grows its adult teeth, you can get it used to the process by gently rubbing its gums with your fingers. If your puppy doesn't allow you to get your hands near its mouth, you can try dipping your fingers in peanut butter or any food that your puppy loves. Once your puppy allows you to insert your finger in its mouth, try massaging the gums. After a couple of times, you can use a small, soft toothbrush that fits on your fingertip and add peanut butter or other tasty dips. When you feel that your puppy is comfortable with this process as well, you can start adding some dog-friendly toothpaste onto the soft brush so it can get used to the flavor.

Dental care routine
Once your puppy has all its adult teeth, you can use a professional dog's toothbrush and start brushing its teeth once a week, and then make it three to four times a week. This way, you can avoid all dental problems and guarantee that your dog has healthy teeth and gums. And just like us, dogs need dental check-ups at least twice a year to make sure that their teeth don't need cleaning or have any other problems.

What tools to get
Not all dogs are the same; what can work for one dog might not work for another. That's why the toothbrushing process is all about trial and error. You will need to try out several types of toothbrushes and toothpaste until you find the one that your puppy loves and feels comfortable with. There is a lot of variety when it comes to toothbrushes. You will find soft brushes, tiny finger toothbrushes, and regular ones. Each one is for a specific size and age, which means that

you'll probably change the toothbrush a lot in the first six to eight months.

The best time to start brushing your pup's teeth is when it has all its adult teeth. However, before that, you can start familiarizing it with the process. It's never too late to start adding dental care to your grooming routine, but starting at an early stage can make it way easier for both of you. If you feel that your puppy has stinky breath, then a visit to the vet is mandatory, because this might indicate dental issues. The sooner you detect the problem, the easier it is to fix it.

Ear Cleaning

Many dogs enjoy having their ears rubbed and massaged, but some dogs might feel threatened when someone touches their ears. To make sure that your puppy allows you to touch its ears, start getting it used to this once you bring it home. This part is very important because you will need your puppy to sit without moving while you're cleaning its ears. Ear cleaning may not be a priority to many dog owners, but it's essential as it can prevent a lot of infections and health issues.

Some dogs need regular cleaning more than others, especially dogs with long, floppy ears, as this shape doesn't allow for enough airflow into the ear canal. These breeds are more prone to ear infections and wax buildup than other dogs. However, no matter what breed you have, you should clean and check your puppy's ears regularly.

Ear anatomy
Before you start cleaning, you should be familiar with your puppy's ears to avoid any damages. The visible outer flap of the ear is called the pinna. In some dogs, it could stand up straight, and others may have floppy ears. When you look inside your puppy's ear, you will find the external canal, which is the visible ear opening, covered in skin, and has flexible tissues. You will see that the external canal moves toward the vertical and horizontal canal, and it contains glands, wax, and oils. The external canal ends at the eardrum, the thin layer of tissues, and the middle and inner ear come after the eardrum. Any damage to the eardrum, and the middle or inner ear can cause serious problems to your puppy and may affect its hearing and balance.
What to use

To clean your puppy's ears, you will need a cleaning solution. You can purchase the solution from a pet shop or ask your vet for their recommendation depending on your puppy's breed and age. You can't use cleaning solutions designed for humans, as they may damage your pup's ears. Cleaning solutions that contain alcohol or hydrogen peroxide may cause ear problems.

Cleaning the ears
Get your pup to sit and give it a treat. After that, start massaging its ears and add a few drops of the cleaning solution to fill the ear canal. For twenty seconds after adding the ear solution, gently massage the ears.
Remove your hands from your pup's ears and let it shake its head if it wants while holding up a towel to prevent the solution from flying everywhere. Use a cotton ball to clean the outer parts of the ear.

Regular ear cleaning will help you detect ear infections or other health issues before they cause any severe problems. If you find that your puppy's ears are too red or have a bad smell, then a visit to the vet is a must, as this might indicate a serious problem. If you regularly massage and clean your puppy's ears, this part of the grooming process will only take a few minutes.

Nail Trimming

If your puppy spends a lot of time outside and regularly walks on a hard surface like concrete, you won't need to trim its nails too often, as the hard surface will do that job. However, if it spends most of its time indoors or in a garden, you will need to trim its nails at least once a month. Untrimmed nails can be uncomfortable for your puppy, and sometimes it might cause pain. If your dog's nails are too long, they might start scratching furniture, floors, and even people. Nail trimming is essential because long nails might cause puppies' toes to spread, which can affect the ankle joints and might cause walking problems in the future.

Many dog owners can't get their dogs to sit for nail trimming, and they consider it the hardest part of the grooming process. But if you include it in the grooming routine as soon as you bring your puppy home, it could be easy and comfortable both for you and your puppy.

Important points
Before you begin the trimming process, you should make sure that you have the right clippers for your pup's size and breed. You first need to understand that your puppy's nails are made of two parts, the nail itself and the quick. The quick is the pink part at the beginning of the nail. While cutting the nails, you must avoid that pink part because it can result in bleeding and be a very painful experience for your puppy.

Preparation
Before cutting your puppy's nails, sit beside it and give it a lot of praise and affection. Sitting in front of your dog can be disturbing for it. When it's all calm and comfortable, start by holding the foot firmly without squeezing it. Place its paw in your hand and hold each toe you're willing to trim with your index finger and thumb. Hold the clipper in your other hand in order to be able to handle your puppy.

Clipping
You can start by clipping the tips of the nails. That way, you can be more confident about the process and let your puppy get familiar and comfortable with it.

After clipping the tips, you can start cutting the nail itself, avoiding the quick.

Once you're done with this process, give your puppy treats and praise so that it knows that it did something good. This way, the clipping session can go smoother the next time.

If your puppy starts pulling its paws away from you, give it a firm "stay" command and praise it afterward if it obeys.

It's preferable to start nail trimming at an early age to give your puppy some time to get comfortable with it. You can repeat it once a week until your dog gets used to it completely. If you're not able to cut all the nails at the same time, you can trim one paw at a time and squeeze some playtime and praise in between each. By doing this, you will make your pup enjoy this grooming process. Some puppies' nails are brown, black, or gray, which makes it hard to spot the quick. In that case, you can cut the tips only, or you can take your dog to a professional groomer to be on the safe side.

Chapter 6: Doctor at Home

It's a terrible feeling when you can sense that your puppy isn't being itself but you're not sure how serious its condition is or what you can do to help. This is why it's important to know how to read your dog's vitals. The more you know about what's normal for your pup, the quicker you can tell when something isn't quite right with it.

Knowing how to check your dog's vital signs enables you to evaluate its degree of pain, injury, or illness and accordingly get it the help it needs.

CRT
One of the basic vital signs you need to check is your dog's capillary refill time (CRT). Below, we'll explain what CRT is, why it's important, and how you can check it.

What is CRT?
Capillary refill time or CRT is the measure of a dog's blood flow, including its blood circulation and perfusion. The normal time it takes for the capillaries to refill in a healthy dog is under two seconds. A prolonged CRT can indicate blood flow irregularities, meaning that the heart isn't

able to pump the blood to some tissues appropriately.

This can occur if your pup is in or going into shock or if it's suffering from heart disease. Checking your dog's CRT is a fast and easy process that can alert you if your pet has a serious condition.

How to check your puppy's CRT
To check your puppy's CRT, carefully lift its lips, and then using your thumb or index finger, apply pressure to the gums just above or below a tooth until the gum turns white. Once the gum under your finger has been blanched out, release the pressure and measure how long it takes for the color to return. For a healthy pup, a normal CRT is around one or two seconds.

If your dog's CRT is longer than two seconds, it might need immediate veterinary care. If that's the case, cover your pup with a light blanket while transporting it to preserve body heat. Slightly elevate its hindquarters (unless it's suffering from a bleeding injury) to promote circulation to its vital organs.

It's worth mentioning that a normal CRT isn't necessarily proof of overall good health, but an abnormal one is definitely an indication that something is wrong.

Why should you measure it?

In addition to being an indicator of your dog's cardiac health, checking its CRT allows you to get a good look at its gums. Gum color can provide insight into your pup's overall health. Unless it has naturally dark gums, pink gums typically reflect normal health. If your puppy's gums are pale, white, yellow, blue, or gray, immediate professional care should be sought.

There's no need to wait for a severe symptom to occur before you start worrying about your dog's well-being. We strongly advise you to assess your dog's vitals frequently, including its CRT. And remember, when in doubt, it's always better to have your puppy checked by a vet immediately.

Checking Temperature

Your puppy's temperature is a good indicator of its overall health. It's one of the first things your veterinarian will check when you take your dog for a regular visit. To give your fur baby the best care possible, it's important that you know how to check its temperature, how to interpret the reading, and how to act if it's higher or lower than normal.

What's a puppy's normal temperature?

Normal body temperature can vary from one puppy to another, which is why taking your dog's temperature is important as it tells you what your puppy's "normal" is. Generally, the average temperature for newborn puppies falls between 95° and 99°F. At around three weeks old, your puppy's temperature should range from 97° to 100°F, and after the fourth week, it should have the normal body temperature of an adult dog, which is usually between 99.5° and 102.5°F.

Body temperature over 104°F or under 99°F is an indication of an emergency situation. Extremely high or low temperatures can be fatal for puppies if not treated. So if you take your puppy's temperature and the reading appears to be dangerously high or low, seek veterinary care immediately.

How to check your puppy's temperature

A popular myth surrounding the body temperature of dogs is that you can tell if they have a fever by feeling their noses. If it's cool and wet, then the dog's temperature is normal, but if it's hot and dry, then it has a fever. This is completely wrong; the only accurate way to check your dog's temperature is by using a thermometer.

Ear and mouth temperatures are unreliable in dogs, which means that you'll need a digital or a bulb rectal thermometer to get an accurate reading. As unpleasant as it may sound, many dogs eventually learn really well how to tolerate having their rectal temperature taken. However, until your pup gets used to it, it might be easier if you get another person to help you hold your dog in place while you take its temperature.
The procedure will take around a minute, so make sure that your dog is comfortable in its standing position before you start.
Besides the thermometer, you will also need baby oil, mineral oil, or petroleum jelly to lubricate the tip of the thermometer.

To measure the pup's temperature, lift its tail and gently but quickly insert the lubricated thermometer about an inch into its rectum. Press the start button on your digital thermometer and hold it in place until you hear the beep that signals completion. If you're using a bulb thermometer, you won't have to press a button, but you will need to shake down the thermometer until it reads about 96°F before you use it. After you're done with the thermometer, be sure to clean it using rubbing alcohol or a suitable, dog-friendly disinfectant.

Checking your puppy's temperature should be a normal part of your routine. Once you manage to hold your dog in place, taking its temperature will be quite simple. Just bear in mind that if your puppy has a fever, do not, under any circumstances, give it medication at home without consulting your vet. Human medication can be poisonous to dogs and cause severe illness or even death.

Understanding Bowel Movements

Bowel movement isn't a pleasant topic to talk about but it's a very important one; your puppy's stool is a good indicator of its overall health. Keeping an eye on your dog's poop can help you ensure its well-being and alert you in case of a health problem. To better monitor your pet's health, you must understand the signs that differentiate between healthy and unhealthy dog poop.

What should healthy poop look like?
When picking up after your dog, there are four main characteristics to look for in its poop: color, content, consistency, and coating. The color of healthy stool should be chocolate brown and there shouldn't be any visible content in it. As for the consistency, your puppy's stool should be firm and a little moist, like play-dough. Ideally, your pup's stool would be log-shaped with little cracks in it and no coating on it at all. So, if your puppy has medium-brown, semi-firm, coating-free poop with nothing sticking out of it, you have nothing to worry about.

How does your puppy's diet affect its bowel movement?
The volume and odor of the stool are also important to note. Puppies who eat only processed kibble typically excrete large quantities of stinking poop. This is because many dog food manufacturers add high amounts of fiber to their products and your puppy can't process all these nutrients so instead of metabolizing them, its body pushes them out, producing high volume with a strong odor.

Dogs who eat raw and homemade food typically produce significantly smaller stool with a much weaker smell, but if the raw diet is too high in calcium, your puppy may pass white, chalky feces or even suffer from constipation.

As you can see, what constitutes "normal" poop may vary depending on the pup's diet among other factors. This is why it's important to pay attention to what your dog's stool usually looks and smells like so you'll be immediately aware of any signs of potential health problems.

The most common poop abnormalities

Diarrhea is a common sign of a potential health problem in puppies. The causes of diarrhea typically include viral and bacterial infections, intestinal parasites, food intolerance, allergies, and inflammatory bowel disease. In the case of large bowel inflammation, diarrhea is often accompanied by a coating of mucus. Another common abnormality is soft stool with no visible blood or mucus. This is usually a result of either a dietary change or irregular eating. Regardless of the stool's consistency, the presence of red streaks or fresh blood is almost always a sign of a serious health problem that requires immediate attention.

When it comes to your puppy's overall health, what they excrete is as important as what they ingest, and since your furry friend can't tell you when they have a stomach ache or some other digestive problem, it's up to you to stay alert for signs of trouble. So, bring your tolerance levels up and look for the for Cs in your dog's stool: color, content, consistency, and coating.

Wound Care

Puppies are naturally playful, energetic and inquisitive; all these traits may lead to accidents resulting in cuts and scrapes at some point in their life. Cleaning the wound properly will prevent infection and help your dog heal quickly if you cover all your bases. Understanding how to assess wounds and treat them is essential for your pup's health.

Stopping the bleeding

Any shallow wound, whether bleeding or not, will require immediate attention to ensure it doesn't get infected. Once you realize your puppy has a wound, the first step is to stop the bleeding. Apply pressure on the wound with a gauze tape or a cloth for a bigger cut.

Cleaning the wound

Once the bleeding has stopped, you need to flush out the wound as soon as possible. You will need to use a saline solution as a first step. You can either use a store-bought saline solution—such as contact lens solution if you have it on hand—or you can make some at home. To make the saline solution, add two teaspoons of salt to one cup of warm water and stir until completely dissolved.

To use the solution, its best to use a syringe or baster and squirt a large volume of the liquid to bathe or drown the wound in. This is both to disinfect the wound and to clean out any bacteria and debris that might not be noticeable. Keep washing the wound until the tissue is clear and glistening. If the wound is on your pup's tail or paw, keep the solution in a bowl and soak the injured paw or tail for three to five minutes and then pat dry gently.

What to use

Depending on the severity of the wound, you may want to use a disinfectant as a final rinse or soak. You can dilute a capful of betadine or chlorhexidine in a cup of warm water to use for this purpose.

Unless instructed by your vet, never use hydrogen peroxide, harsh soaps or shampoos, rubbing alcohol, oils, or any other product to clean an open wound, as they may contain substances that are toxic to your puppy or may irritate the wound and inflame it further.

Drying the wound

Once you are sure the wound is clean, you need to dry it. It's a good idea to use a gauze pad because it won't leave any fragments in the wound, but any clean and lint-free material will be fine. Pat the wound gently to avoid causing more pain or injury, then bandage the wound to keep your puppy from licking it. Use a bandage tape around the gauze to hold it in place.

Following up

After you've taken all these steps, it's a good idea to keep checking on the wound daily to see how it is healing. If it seems to be going ok, then just continue to change the bandages regularly until the wound is completely healed. However, if the wound does not close, or starts to emit any smell, you have to contact your veterinarian immediately.

It's important to understand that for small wounds such as scratches and minor cuts, you can easily take care of your puppy at home. However, for any other type of injury that fully penetrates the skin such as bite wounds, deep gashing wounds, or bruises that won't heal, your puppy should receive immediate veterinary attention.

Giving Pills to Your Puppy
Many people think that it's practically impossible to give their pet its pills. And they have all the right to feel this way; after all, you might end up chasing your puppy all around the house. This is when you start to look for new and practical ways to give your little pooch its meds. Thankfully, there are plenty of those you can try—if one doesn't work, the next surely will.

Go old school
If your little puppy is an easygoing sweetheart, you can simply give it the pill as is. All you need to do is tilt back its head to face the ceiling, then gently open its mouth. After that, you push the pill to the back of its tongue and stroke its throat until you make sure that the pill is swallowed. To double-check, you can give your pup some water in order to be sure that the pill does not get stuck in its throat.

Sneak it in soft or sticky food

Trick 101 to giving your puppy its pills is through hiding one in its food. Try sticking the pill in a meatball or a dollop of peanut butter and your pet will swallow it without even noticing that it's there. The good thing about this trick is that there are many types of sticky and soft foods for you to hide the pill in—so you can experiment until you find the one thing that your puppy never seems to refuse.

Try out food pockets
This trick is somewhat similar to the previous one. However, it is mainly used for picky dogs that are very particular about what they eat. These pets are very intelligent and can easily realize that there is a hidden pill in their food. They end up eating around the pill and leave the rest. In this case, you can start trying out food pockets; they have the right texture and consistency that will trick your puppy into swallowing the pills.

Use a pill device
Pill devices are one of the very helpful tools created for pets. Using one helps you avoid the hassle of getting your hand bitten just because your puppy is refusing to take its meds and starting to get a little too agitated. All you need

to do to use this device is to simply place it as close as you can to the puppy's throat, and drop the pill. After that, close its jaws and gently stroke its throat downwards to make sure that swallows it.

Puppies are adorable indeed, but they are very smart as well. So, don't underestimate how tricky it can be to convince them to do something they don't want to. However, giving them the right medication can be of vital importance, so it's best to start familiarizing them with this process early on. This is why you need to make sure that you stay calm and be persistent each time you give your dog a pill—when it knows there's nothing to be afraid of, it'll eventually be happy to cooperate.

Common Illnesses

Puppies can suffer from a lot of the same illnesses and health conditions as adult dogs, but because of their size and age, these illnesses can be a lot more serious in their case. They are more prone to developing diseases as their bodies are not strong enough to combat viruses and bacteria. Here, we list the most common illnesses that can affect puppies that you have to be aware of and keep an eye out for.

Kennel cough

Also known as infectious tracheobronchitis, this illness is characterized by an aggravating and loud cough. It's very contagious and often contracted from crowded places such as dog kennels or pet stores. If your puppy has it, it will need a visit to the vet as soon as possible to get medical treatment, as untreated kennel cough can develop into deadly pneumonia in puppies. If your pooch is abnormally tired, has a decreased appetite and fever, along with a wheezing cough, then definitely get it checked out. With the right treatment, your puppy should get better within 10 – 14 days.

Canine parvovirus

Another serious illness that is very common among puppies is canine parvovirus (parvo). It typically affects puppies up to four months of age, especially if they haven't received all their vaccinations yet. Parvo is caused by a virus that induces symptoms that start with bloody diarrhea, then it is followed by vomiting, sleepiness, and loss of appetite. If you see any of those symptoms in your puppy, you have to take it to a veterinarian immediately. In this case, your dog will most likely be hospitalized for a few days and then go home with medication to continue treatment.

Canine distemper

Another common disease is distemper, which threatens to affect young puppies that have not yet been vaccinated against it. Unfortunately, puppies who contract this illness are at a high risk of developing permanent neurological damage. Symptoms can include yellow diarrhea, issues with breathing, eye and nasal discharge, and loss of appetite. If your puppy contracts distemper, it will most likely be hospitalized for a few weeks before it can go back home with you.

Hyperglycemia

Especially if you own a toy breed puppy, such as a chihuahua or miniature poodle, you need to be aware that it might be at a high risk of experiencing hyperglycemia during the first year of its life. Toy breeds have tiny stomachs that may not be able to handle long intervals between meals. This causes them to have low blood sugar, and that can have a serious effect on their health—and even become life-threatening. Puppies suffering from hyperglycemia will start being inactive, appear to be spaced out or not focused, and in extreme cases, they will experience seizures and even death. Young puppies need to be fed every four hours on average, and if you feel that your puppy is showing any symptoms of low blood sugar, place a small amount of honey right into its mouth and follow up with a vet appointment right away.

Gastrointestinal issues

Although they're technically not illnesses but rather symptoms, vomiting and diarrhea can be very common indicators of underlying diseases. If your puppy is experiencing either—or both—the first thing to do is rule out a serious case of intestinal parasites. It can also simply be an upset tummy or that your puppy ate too fast or licked something that was not clean. Some puppies might even vomit due to hunger or stress. The severity of GI issues depends on the dog's habits and how long they last. No matter the case, **you have to keep your puppy well hydrated** for the following 12 hours after vomiting or 24 hours after diarrhea. If your pooch does not get better, then a visit to the veterinarian will be required.

These guidelines are meant to help you know when something is wrong, assess how severe the situation is, and help you provide specific, detailed information to your vet. They're by no means a substitute to veterinary care but may prove useful in determining whether or not your pet needs an emergency visit to the vet.

Dealing with Fleas and Ticks

Fleas and ticks are nightmares for dog owners. There are thousands of pests out there, but a handful can be enough to affect your puppy and bring you misery. Although ticks and fleas are year-round pests, owners tend to encounter them the most during warmer months. These tiny parasites not only irritate your dog, but they also transmit disease and infest your home.

If you and your dog are already scratching your heads, we've got you covered with a list of prevention methods and ways to deal with fleas and ticks.

How to know if your puppy has ticks or fleas

Your puppy will probably be constantly scratching and biting itself along the back and the base of its tail if it's infested by fleas.

Because some dogs are allergic to the flea's saliva, a few puppies will show signs of a severe skin reaction from just a single bite. You might also notice brownish-black fleas moving through your puppy's hair or flea dirt on its coat.

The presence of ticks, however, is harder to detect. Your dog may have several of them attached to its skin without showing any symptoms, so it's very important to examine it closely by parting the fur and running your hands through its skin. Pay special attention to your puppy's face, inside the ears, between the toes, as well as the groin area.

Laying their eggs in bushes or dark, sheltered areas, ticks attach themselves to the skin and feed on blood. Their sizes can range from a poppy seed to a raisin, and it's crucial to remove them as soon as possible, as they can transmit serious diseases.

Prevention methods

Fleas and ticks tend to hate sunlight and stick to dark, hidden areas. However, that doesn't mean your energetic puppy that loves playing outside won't need maximum protection. Especially if you live—or go for hikes—in woody areas, you should be extra careful to protect your fur baby.

Make sure your lawn's grass is short to ensure it gets enough sunlight, and clean up woodpiles or fallen leaves regularly to prevent ticks from dwelling there.

For your backyard, you can use nematodes and diatomaceous earth to keep fleas and ticks under control.

Treatment

Even though the preventives will keep the parasites away, you might still need to take more measures to get rid of existing fleas and ticks. The two basic control products are adulticides and insect growth regulators. Adulticides kill adult fleas, whereas the insect growth regulators stop ticks and fleas from maturing. You can also opt for flea shampoos, pills or powders that kill those insects within hours.

Removing ticks will require tweezers, and it can help if your partner holds the dog as you go through the process. Make sure you grab the tick by its head, as close to the skin as possible, or else its body may be crushed all over your dog, sending toxins into its bloodstream. After removing the tick, place it in a jar filled with rubbing alcohol, as your vet might need to identify the specific type of tick that bit your dog in case of a complication.

To get rid of fleas manually, you'll need a flea comb. Comb your dog's hair thoroughly, and if fleas get stuck in the comb's teeth, place them in soapy water for a while to ensure that they're all dead before you discard it.

Keep your home free from fleas and ticks
After you've treated your dog, you'll still want to make sure the fleas and ticks are out of your home. You'll need to wash all the bedding in hot water, apply non-toxic sprays to your yard, vacuum all your carpets and floors and then throw away the vacuum bag, and continue to treat your dog with the monthly preventives. If you have a serious home infestation at hand, you can go for flea bombs or seek professional help.

It hurts to see your pet in pain. If it's going through a pest infestation, it will likely spend hours every day scratching itself and biting at its paws. If it's prone to allergies, flea and tick bites may even lead to a weakened immune system, causing a whole lot of other issues. Luckily, though, with constant care, you can get rid of the nuisance of ticks and fleas, and keep them in check for good.

Vaccinations

As your puppy learns to interact with the world, you'll need to take good care of its physical health, and this includes prevention. You'll need to protect your dog from potentially harmful diseases through vaccinations.

When to consider vaccination

A puppy should ideally start taking vaccines as soon as you get it, unless it's a special case. You'll need to continue with your fur baby's booster shots every three weeks until it is four months of age. Vaccinations normally begin after the puppy has been weaned off by its mother.

Remember to schedule your vaccination appointment during your first veterinarian visit, which should take place sometime around the first week of receiving your new pet.

Core vaccines you cannot skip

Some vaccines are required by all dogs, while some others will depend on your pup's lifestyle. Core vaccinations are vital to your puppy's health and well-being.

Canine distemper

As mentioned before, this severe and dangerous virus affects dogs' nervous, respiratory and gastrointestinal systems, spreading from other infected animals. It can also be transmitted through food or shared equipment. The virus causes discharge from the nose and eyes, coughing, fever, vomiting, seizure, paralysis, diarrhea, and twitching. In the worst cases, it can lead to death. You need to make sure your puppy is vaccinated against this virus at around six weeks of age. Then, your vet will follow up with the vaccines every two to three weeks, until your pup is four months old. A booster shot will be given when your dog turns one.

Canine hepatitis
As a highly contagious virus infection, hepatitis affects the lungs, liver, kidneys, spleen, lungs, and eyes. If infected, your dog will show signs of a fever, vomiting, stomach enlargement, and will feel pain around its liver. The mild forms of the disease can be overcome, but in rare cases, hepatitis can be deadly. Between six and 16 weeks of age, your puppy will receive at least three doses of this vaccine.

Rabies
Rabies is known as a viral disease that harms many mammals and invades their nervous system. This virus causes hallucinations, headaches, anxiety, excessive drooling, paralysis,

fear of water, and death. This type of vaccination is mandatory in most states and is taken seriously.

Canine Parvovirus

Unvaccinated puppies that are less than four months of age are at high risks of getting infected with this virus. It attacks the gastrointestinal system, causing fevers, vomiting and bloody diarrhea.

Non-core vaccines

Non-core vaccines are optional. Where you live and where you travel with your dog will affect the type of shots it will be taking.

Bordetella bronchiseptica

Leading to the disease known as kennel cough, this bacterium is highly infectious, causing vomiting and severe coughing. In some rare cases, it might cause seizures and death. Injectable vaccines and nasal sprays keep this enemy away.

Canine influenza

Affecting the dog's upper respiratory system, this virus is the canine equivalent for the common flu. It causes nasal discharge, a cough and sometimes a mild fever. If your dog tends to have more severe symptoms than usual, you may choose to give it this vaccine as a preventative measure.

Bringing home those soft little balls of fur means you're now responsible for your puppy's life. Your dog will depend on you when it comes to your attention, training and proper veterinary care. It may sound intimidating at first, but by following the right steps, you won't have to worry too much.

Although your dog will need a myriad of check-ups, medications and vaccinations throughout its life, the frequency of these will mostly depend on its lifestyle. Fortunately, the core preventives will be over early on, and in time, you'll be accustomed to the entire schedule.

Still, your loving little fur baby deserves your undivided attention and care—meaning that you'll have to get used to doing a significant amount of research on canine health. Because it's hard to keep track of these things on your own, make sure you regularly consult a vet for extra help with your puppy's physical health.

Conclusion

Not many would argue that dogs are one of the most beautiful creatures in the world. Their kindness, unconditional love, and never-ending loyalty are just heartwarming—plus, there's the fact that they are just adorable. It doesn't matter what breed your dog is; as long as you love it, it will reciprocate like no other creature can, and you will be its entire world for the rest of its life. Raising a dog is a responsibility not everyone is prepared for, much like bringing up kids. This is why it's important to start when they are at a very young age by teaching them basic commands that will make both your lives easier.

Printed in Great Britain
by Amazon